Theology Today

GENERAL EDITOR:

EDWARD YARNOLD, S.J.

No. 10

The Theology of Inspiration

BY

JOHN SCULLION, S.J.

FIDES PUBLISHERS, INC.

NOTRE DAME, INDIANA

Nihil Obstat:
Jeremiah J. O'Sullivan, D.D.
Censor deputatus
22nd October 1970

Imprimatur:
† Cornelius Ep. Corcag. & Ross
29th October 1970

SBN 85342 229 X

CONTENTS

ACKNOWLEDGEMENTS

The Scripture quotations in this publication are from the Revised Standard Version of the Bible, copyrighted 1946 and 1952 by the Division of Christian Education of the National Council of the Churches of Christ in the U.S.A. and used by kind permission. Quotations from The Documents of Vatican II (ed. W.M.Abbott, S.J.) are printed by kind permission of The America Press and Geoffrey Chapman Ltd, London.

ABBREVIATIONS

P.G.	J. P. Migne: *Patrologia Graeca*
P.L.	J. P. Migne: *Patrologia Latina*
C.S.E.L.	*Corpus Scriptorum Ecclesiasticorum Latinorum*
Dz	H. Denzinger & A. Schönmetzer, *Enchiridion Symbolorum, Definitionum et Declarationum* (33rd edit., Barcelona etc., 1965)
RSS	*Rome and the Study of Scripture*, Grail Publications, St Meinrad, Indiana, 6th edit., 1958
C.T.S.	Catholic Truth Society, London.

PREFACE

In recent decades great strides have been made in the understanding of the way in which the Bible was written. First, we now know it is necessary to learn all history can teach about the literary forms of biblical times so as to avoid interpreting a statement written in one form as if it belonged to a different genre. Secondly, it now appears that many biblical books were not written from scratch by one author in the shape in which they have come down to us, but are the result of a long and growing oral and written tradition and a process of compilation. Thirdly, the Bible contains contradictions, scientific inaccuracies and factual mistakes.

These three comparatively new insights into the method of composition of the Bible require a corresponding revision in our view of biblical inspiration. The whole evolution of a book, including oral tradition, constituent documents, and final compilation and editing, takes place under the inspiration of the Holy Spirit. Nevertheless the human authors, even though inspired throughout, depended on natural talent and existing sources, and thought in the thoughtforms of their times. Inspiration, then, is certainly not like automatic writing in a trance, in which the writer purports to be a passive and unconscious instrument of a dictating spirit.

Fr Scullion, while examining the recent developments of Catholic thinking about inspiration, formulates his own conclusions on the subject.

E.J.Yarnold, S.J.

INTRODUCTION

The problem of the inspiration of sacred books follows on the belief in a personal God who in some way communicates with his intelligent creature, man. Is there a record of this communication? Israel and the Christian Church has always believed that there is and that God's unfolding of himself to man in history, his revelation, is found in Scripture. The Church believes that God's revelation reached its climax in Jesus Christ and she finds the written record of this in the Bible as a whole.

The Bible is one of the fruits of God's education of his people. It belongs to God that he is faithful and true. The divine pedagogue leads man step by step to the truth and helps him to slough off error. As we read the Bible we experience through the medium of ancient Near Eastern literature this gradual and painful journey towards truth which is expressed in the New Testament in the milieu of Judaeo-Hellenistic literature.

No matter what the experience of the prophet, writer, hagiographer, historiographer, if he wishes to communicate he must speak or write in human language and be bound by its limits. Isaiah, Ezekiel, Paul came face to face with God, however blinding and obscure the confrontation. The many unknown authors of the Old Testament 'historical' books experienced God in their meditation on history and tradition. Their problem was to convey in words of men the word of God.

The books of the Bible were written by men of faith, for people of faith, to deepen faith. The Bible is above all a religious book. It is in this context of faith that we must come to the question of its inspiration.

It is Jewish and Christian belief that the Bible was

written under the special guidance and inflow of the Holy Spirit. The prophet or writer illuminated by the divine light, though by no means necessarily conscious of it, thinks, speaks, moves, writes wholly and completely in a human manner. He remains a man and acts as a man though all the time acted on by the Spirit.

The problem of inspiration, then, is but an aspect of the general problem of divine-human co-operation. One may approach it as a speculative philosopher-theologian or as an exegete-historian who is not unfamiliar with theology and theological method. It is the latter, positive approach that is taken here.

In no branch of knowledge can one neglect the work of those who have gone before. It is necessary then to examine the contributions to the study of the problem made by the man of the past. As the Bible had its origin in the people of God and in the Church of God, it is the Church's book. We must know what the Church has had to say about her book. Our method will be to trace the history of inspiration from the Old and New Testaments through the documents of the Church and then see how theologians and exegetes have commented on and explained this data. We will then look at the development of the Bible historically and see how God 'condescended' to adapt his communication of himself, his truth, within the shackling limits of time-conditioned man. This truth can and must be expressed in ways ever ancient and ever new.

CHAPTER 1

GOD, THE AUTHOR OF SCRIPTURE

'Inspiration' from the Old Testament to the New Testament

(a) *The Old Testament*

The people of the Old Testament believed that God guided them through his Spirit. They believed that the great figures who formed their traditions, Abraham, Moses, the prophets, acted and spoke under the Spirit. Abraham was God's friend (Is 41.8); God appeared to him at Mamre (Gen 18.1). Moses received the revelation of the divine name (Ex 3.1-15) and God spoke to him face to face (Num 12.4-8). The Spirit of the Lord came upon the prophet who spoke at the end of the exile (Is 61.1). And when 'the Lord God has spoken, who can but prophesy?' (Amos 3.8).

The book of Exodus is witness to the belief that the Torah, the Law or teaching, came directly from God to the mediator Moses and thence to Israel (Ex 19.1-25; 24.1-18). The priests of Israel guarded and expounded the Torah and gave 'priestly instruction' concerning morality and liturgical practice. 'For the lips of a priest should guard knowledge, and men should seek instruction *(torah)* from his mouth, for he is the messenger of the Lord of hosts' (Mal 2.7). The priests, as preservers and interpreters, were the heirs of Moses.

God is also the source and inspirer of wisdom in Israel. 'The fear of the Lord is the beginning of knowledge' (Prov 1.7). That is, knowledge or wisdom is essentially reverential respect before God. And man cannot discover this by his own study (cf. Job 28).

The breath of the Spirit in the Old Testament moved

men to speak, not necessarily to write, though even in the pre-exilic period we must recognize that much was written.

(b) *Judaism*

It was in the five hundred years which we call the period of Judaism, 400 B.C. – 100 A.D. (approx.) that a belief in the divine origin of the sacred books appeared. Before this, in 621 B.C., Josiah had adopted the 'book of the Covenant' (2 Kings 23.1-2). Later, after the return and the rebuilding of the Temple and the walls of Jerusalem, Ezra read to the whole people from 'the book of the law of Moses which God had given to Israel' (Neh 8.1ff.). In the time of the Maccabees, about the middle of the second century B.C., Jonathan could write in a letter that 'we have as an encouragement the holy books which are in our hands' (1 Mac 12.9). We have not sufficient information to trace the growth and development of a firm belief in the divine origin of the sacred books. Our resources are too sparse. The Greek translator of the *Wisdom of Ben Sirach (Ecclesiasticus)* writing about 117 B.C. – he came to Egypt in the thirty-eighth year of Ptolemy VII, Euergetes II, 170-117 B.C. – knows the division of the books that are sacred into 'the law itself, the prophecies, and the rest of the books...' (Prologue).

The people of Israel became known as the people of the book because of the great respect they had for the written Law. It was to the Law, the Torah (Pentateuch) that they ascribed the highest degree of inspiration. Every jot and tittle of it had been caused by God. One tradition tells that the Torah had been caused by God before the foundation of the world and had in some way been literally revealed to Moses. He wrote the whole of the Torah at God's dictation, the last eight verses in tears. The prophets and the writings were written under the divine influence, but this influence did not extend to the same intimate detail as in the Torah. Another tradition

12

is preserved in 2 Esdras 14.18-48 (about 100 A.D.). All the manuscripts of the sacred books had been lost when Jerusalem was destroyed. Ezra was taken into a trance and in it he dictated to his five scribes uninterruptedly for forty days and nights the twenty-four sacred books and some seventy others for the initiated. Judaism attributed the books or groups of books to individual great names, Moses, Joshua, Samuel, David, Solomon and the great prophets. All of these men were under the Spirit, and so the books were inspired. Judaism believed that the books of the Old Testament were from God, that is that they were inspired by his Spirit. It is this belief that became part of the Christian faith.

(c) *The New Testament*
The New Testament continually cites the Old Testament and affirms its divine origin. 'It is written' is a typical way in which the rabbis referred to their sacred books. Jesus takes up the phrase (e.g., Matt 4.4ff.), as does Peter in reference to the Psalms (Acts 1.20). God spoke through David (Acts 4.25); 'The Holy Spirit was right in saying to your Fathers through Isaiah the prophet...' (Acts 28.25). God and Scripture are sometimes interchanged: 'And the scripture... preached the gospel beforehand to Abraham...' (Gal 3.8; cf. Gen 12.3); '...as God said...' (2 Cor 6.16; Heb 1.5-7); 'The Holy Spirit says...' (Heb 3.7; 10.15). So long as the words are in the Old Testament they may be attributed to God, the Holy Spirit or the Scripture without distinction. Passages from the Old Testament are 'the oracles of God' (Rom 3.2).

There are two classical texts that speak of God's action in the formation of the Old Testament:
i) 2 Tim 3.14-17:
But as for you, continue in what you have learned and have firmly believed, knowing from whom you learned it and how from childhood you have

been acquainted with the sacred writings which are able to instruct you for salvation through faith in Christ Jesus. All scripture *(pasa graphe)* is inspired *(theopneustos)* by God and profitable for teaching, for reproof, for correction and for training in righteousness, that the man of God may be complete, equipped for every good work.

'All scripture...'; the word *graphe* is used in the New Testament of a book or of a passage of Scripture or, with the article, *he graphe,* of entire Scripture. The plural *hai graphai* also refers to the entire collection. The translation of the words *pasa graphe* could be 'all Scripture' or 'every (passage of) Scripture.' As there is no definite article, it is preferable to render in a distributive sense 'every scripture.' The adjective *theopneustos,* inspired, is not found elsewhere in the New Testament. In extrabiblical literature it is rather rare, occurring for example in Plutarch, *Mor.* 904 F, also in Pseudo-Phocylides, Vettius Valens and the Sibylline Oracles. The context in each case requires a passive sense. Theoretically one could translate it actively, 'breathing God', but usage points to the passive rendering. The passage speaks clearly of the divine origin of Scripture.

ii) 2 Pet 1.19-21:

And we have the prophetic word made more sure. You will do well to pay attention to this as to a lamp shining in a dark place, until the day dawns and the morning star rises in your hearts. First of all you must understand this, that no prophecy of scripture is a matter of one's own interpretation, because no prophecy ever came by the impulse of man, but men moved by the Holy Spirit spoke from God.

The context is that prophetic discourse is guaranteed by the witness given to Jesus at his baptism (vv. 17-18). Throughout the passage there is a play on the Greek word *pherein,* bear, carry, move. The voice was borne from heaven and we heard it borne (vv. 17-18). Prophecy is not borne by the will of man, but men who are borne by the Spirit have spoken. The words 'prophecy of Scripture' could refer to the whole of the Old Testament or merely to the prophetic books. However, it seems to be even more restricted. It probably refers to the prophetic office and the work of the prophet himself. He often has to interpret a sign, a vision, a dream. This he does, not of himself, 'of one's own interpretation', but because he is borne by the Spirit. It is not easy to extend the text beyond the realm of prophetic interpretation.

Another text in the same letter of Peter deserves comment. The writer mentions 'our beloved brother Paul' who 'wrote to you according to the wisdom given him... there are some things in them hard to understand, which the ignorant and unstable twist to their own destruction, as they do the other scriptures' (2 Pet 3.14-16). Neither here nor anywhere else does the New Testament claim to be itself inspired. But the author of 2 Peter sets Paul's letters with 'the other scriptures', seemingly putting them with the Old Testament.

If then God is the origin, source, moving force in the formation of the Scriptures, he can in some way be called the author of Scripture. It is this phrase that we must now discuss.

God, Author of Scripture, in tradition and Church documents

God is called the author of Scripture. The phrase has a long history. It first occurs in official documents among some *Ancient Statutes of the Church* which were assembled in the South of France (*Gallia Narbonensis*) in the middle or towards the end of the fifth century. The *Statutes* are not conciliar documents. They prescribe a profession of faith which is to precede ordination as

15

bishop. After professing his belief in the Trinity, the incarnation, death and resurrection of the Son, the candidate is to be asked if he believes that 'there is one and the same author and God of the New and Old Testament, that is, of the Law and Prophets and Apostles' (Dz 325). The origin of the formula is uncertain. As early as the second and third centuries the terminology of the *Statutes,* apart from the word 'author', is found in Origen and Tertullian. Origen in a controversial passage speaks of the writings of the New and Old Testaments as being from the one God (PG 11. 281).

The phrase 'God, author of the Old Testament' was in use in Manichean circles in Augustine's time. In the year 394 Augustine himself could write of 'venerating God as the author of both Testaments', and again 'Everything in both the Old and New Testament has been written down and commended by the one Holy Spirit' (PL 42, 157; CSEL 25, 163, 22-26). Ambrose speaks of the Word of God as the 'author of knowledge' and says that because the precepts and events of the Old and New Testaments agree, it is clear that they have one author (CSEL 62, 188, 18-189, 7). Both Ambrose and Augustine use the phrase 'one author of both testaments'. We can say with certainty that at the end of the fourth century the phrase 'God, author of Scripture' was known and in theological use. It seems to have been forged in a period of controversy with the Manicheans. The word author (*auctor)* does not appear in this context before this date. *Auctor,* author, has many meanings in Latin: it means producer, one who effects something, source and origin. Livy speaks of a certain king as *auctor templi,* one who had a temple erected; Suetonius speaks of the 'author of the human race'. The phrase *auctore me* is rendered 'at my suggestion', and *auctor fui ego ut patres pontem faciendum curarent,* 'I moved the motion that the senate see to the construction of a bridge.' The word *auctor* is used, too, in its modern sense of 'author'. At the beginning of the controversy with the Manicheans 'author' was used to describe God as the source and origin of the old and new testaments, of the old and new economies of salvation, then as the source and origin of the books which contained them.

The words of the *Ancient Statutes of the Church* are resumed and slightly, though not notably, expanded in the profession of faith which Leo IX exchanged with Peter, Patriarch of Antioch, in 1053. 'I believe too that there is one author of the New and Old Testament, the Law and Prophets and Apostles, namely the God and Lord almighty' (Dz 685). The profession of faith which Innocent III demanded of the Waldensian converts in 1208 repeats substantially the formula of the *Statutes* (Dz 790). Over half a century later, in 1274, the Second Council of Lyons received and accepted the profession of faith of the Eastern emperor, Michael Palaeologos to Gregory X, repeating almost verbatim – one conjunction is changed – the sentence cited above from Peter of Antioch's profession (Dz 854). But there is an indication of the sense in which the word *auctor* is understood. The Greek version renders it by *archegos* which means leader, ruler, one who begins something, instigator, originator, founder. God then is the source, origin, initiator, be the words understood ever so widely, of both testaments. It was left to the Council of Florence in its Decree for the Jacobites, 1442, to make a further original and official contribution to the notion of God-author. The Catholic Church, the decree proceeds, acknowledges one and the same God as author of both testaments. The reason is then given: 'because the holy men of both testaments spoke under the inspiration of the same Holy Spirit.' God is the author because he inspires through the Spirit. This council is the first to link author and inspiration. The paragraph then enumerates the books belonging to the Canon and concludes with the sentence: 'Wherefore (the Church) condemns the raving of the Manicheans

17

who have laid down two first principles, one of the visible, the other of the invisible; they said that there was one God of the New Testament and another of the Old' (Dz 1334). The general context is still polemical, but an advance has been made by joining author and inspiration.

The purpose of the Decree of the Council of Trent concerning the sacred books and the traditions to be accepted was that the gospel be preserved in the Church in its purity. Christ himself had promulgated the gospel and had ordered his apostles to preach it to every creature as the source of all salutary truth and moral discipline:

> (The Council perceives that) this truth and discipline is contained in written books and unwritten traditions which the apostles received from the lips of Christ himself or from the prompting *(dictante)* of the Holy Spirit, and handed on so that they have come down to us. Following therefore the example of the Fathers who maintained the truth *(Patrum orthodoxorum),* the Council receives and venerates with equal devotion and filial reverence all books of both the Old and New Testament, since God is the one author of both, as well as the traditions themselves pertaining to faith and moral conduct *(mores),* as coming from the mouth of Christ or as prompted by *(dictante)* the Holy Spirit and preserved by unbroken succession in the Catholic Church. The Council has decided that a list of the sacred books be appended to this decree so that no doubt can arise as to what books it accepts (Dz 1501).

There follows a list of the books of the Old and New Testaments with a paragraph condemning those who do not accept as sacred and canonical the books, wholly and with all parts, that are contained in the traditional and ancient Latin Vulgate together with the traditions described. The tenor of the decree is clear: the message of the gospel is contained in writings and in genuine apostolic traditions; both are to be accepted, the writings, because God is their author, the traditions, because the Holy Spirit made them known to the apostles. There is no advance on the decree of Florence; author and inspiration are not linked. The decree speaks of traditions that have come to the apostles at the 'dictation' of the Holy Spirit, or that have been 'dictated' by the Spirit. We are familiar with the teacher giving a dictation to a class of children, with the business executive dictating a letter to his secretary. The children and the secretary are to do no more nor less than receive and commit accurately to writing what has been spoken to them. It would be incorrect to impose this restricted modern meaning on the decree of Trent. The word *dictare* means not only 'to speak slowly what another is to write down' but also 'to compose, freely prescribe, teach, urge, suggest, enunciate'. It would be a caricature of Trent and of tradition to understand the word woodenly as a passive dictation of the very words of God.

The First Vatican Council, 1870, spoke of revelation in the same way as Trent, quoting the opening words of the paragraph cited above. The decree draws attention to two errors: the Church does not consider the books of the Bible to be holy and canonical (1) because composed by mere human endeavour she has subsequently approved them by her authority, (2) for the mere reason that they contain revelation without error. She maintains that they are sacred and canonical 'because, written under the inspiration of the Holy Spirit, they have God as author and as such have been handed on to the Church' (Dz 3006). Putting the paragraph in logical order we have: (1) there are books which were written under the inspiring breath of the Holy Spirit; (2) these books, therefore, have God as their author; (3) for this reason the Church regards them as holy and canonical. God is the author of the books of the Bible because he inspires them through the Holy Spirit. The formula 'God is the author of Scripture' means nothing else than that the books of the Old and New Testaments are inspired by one and the same God. 'Author' in this context expresses inspiration. In the history of official ecclesiastical documents up to Vatican I, the phrase 'God is the author of both testaments' first meant that God is the source and cause of both covenants; then that he is the source and cause of the books which record the message of these covenants; finally that God through the inspiring breath of the Spirit was at work in forming these books. Hence he is the author. The phrase 'God is author' expresses inspiration.

It is not as if the teaching authority of the Church awoke from time to time to speak of God as author and of inspiration. She was always conscious of their divine origin. The same Spirit who speaks through the teaching authority also works in and speaks through the members. Councils, be they ecumenical or regional, and Popes resume what has become current theological thinking through the writings and discussions of doctors and theologians. This is the case with the notions of 'author' and 'inspiration'. We have seen that Augustine and Ambrose spoke of God as author of both testaments. Before them Origen and Tertullian had used similar terms. Instead of the word 'inspire' some Fathers spoke of God dictating (*hypagoreuein, dictare*) a word which the Rabbis used reserve for the Torah. So John Chrysostom (PG 51. 187), Gregory the Great (PL 75. 517), Augustine (PL 34. 1070), Isidore of Seville (PL 83. 750). This usage has been preserved in the Church and appears in the Council of Trent and in the biblical encyclicals of Leo XIII and Benedict XV. The term is a broad one. Gregory of Nazianzus can see the inspiration of God in the sermons of Basil; Augustine writes to Jerome that in scriptural matters the Holy Spirit not merely gives him (Jerome) great gifts, but even dictates to him (PL 33. 276). Both the Eastern and Western Fathers speak of the Scriptures as written by the Holy Spirit. John Chrysostom describes them as letters from our homeland, from the heavenly Father (PG 53. 27). Augustine uses the example of the Mystical Body to show that God wrote the Scriptures: Christ, by the humanity he assumed, is head of his disciples, head of his body of which they are members. 'Therefore when they wrote what he did and said, it must not be said that he did not write, in as much as his members produced what they knew at the dictation of the head' (PL 34. 1070). The Church of the Fathers was profoundly and widely convinced that the Scriptures had God as their source and author. The expression 'author' emphasizes the supernatural provenance of the books of the Bible rather than the precise idea of literary author (Bishop B.C. Butler).

Documents of Leo XIII, Benedict XV, Pius XII

A vigorous theological debate on the nature of inspiration followed the First Vatican Council to which Cardinal Franzelin, Cardinal Newman, Msgr d'Hulst and Fr M-J. Lagrange made distinct contributions. Into this debate came the encyclical *Providentissimus Deus* of Leo XIII. In the context of inerrancy the Pope gave the fullest description of inspiration hitherto found in an official document. After rejecting the opinion that the Holy Spirit took men as his instruments for writing in such a way that error might come from the inspired writers though not from the primary author, he continues:

He (the Holy Spirit) so stirred and moved them to write by a supernatural power, he so stood by them while they were writing, that they correctly understood, willed to write down faithfully and expressed aptly and with infallible truth all that and

21

only that which he ordered them to write. Otherwise he would not be the author of the whole of Sacred Scripture (Dz 3293).

The Pope did not identify himself with any particular theological school. He made it clear that the notion of inspiration must include (1) an impulse to write, (2) a constant divine assistance in the writer's thought-process, intention and mode of expression. This constant assistance or influence must always be there, but it need not be the same for every writer in every case. The writer may be moved to consign to writing revelation given to himself personally or to others, his own or another's theological reflection on the problems of life or the events of history; he may be moved to record the traditions of his people worked over and reflected upon during the centuries, their life of prayer as expressed in the Psalms continually recited, interpreted and adapted, their wise saws drawn from practical experience and their wisdom-tradition. God is active as the principal agent in all the essential operations that go to form a book. This is necessary if he is to be the author of the book. Benedict XV repeats this teaching in his encyclical *Spiritus Paraclitus,* 1920, which commemorates the fifteenth centenary of the death of St Jerome. The teaching is that the Holy Spirit is constantly present influencing the writer the whole time he is composing his book. Benedict resumes and approves Jerome's teaching that the books of Scripture were composed 'at the inspiration or instigation or urging *(insinuante)* or even dictation of the Holy Spirit; they were even written and published by him' (Dz 3650ff.). Pius XII in *Divino Afflante Spiritu,* 1943, takes for granted the teaching of his predecessors on inspiration. He draws attention to the advance made in explaining the nature and effects of inspiration by following the teaching of St Thomas on instrumentality. Using the classical example of the craftsman carving with his knife, St Thomas shows that the effect, namely the wooden statue, comes wholly from the knife, the instrument, and wholly from the workman, the principal cause. It belongs to the knife to cut and carve, to the craftsman to cut and carve in this or that way. So the total effect is from both, but under different aspects. There is nothing that the knife has not caused, nothing that the craftsman has not caused, yet each has done something that the other could not do alone. There is complete subordination. But when God 'writes' with man, he writes with a unique instrument, one endowed with intellect and free will. God respects the whole human person with all his faculties, he takes man just as he is in a certain place at a certain time, with his cultural and moral and religious developments and limitations, with all his prejudices and short-comings. The mystery lies ultimately in this, that the book is wholly God's and wholly man's.

Such then is the scriptural and traditional matter on which the theologian has to work in elaborating his explanation of the divine inspiration of the sacred books. Some of these explanations we must now examine.

CHAPTER 2

THEORIES OF INSPIRATION

The Tübingen Theologians

In the first half of the nineteenth century the most influential and constructive Catholic school of theology was at Schwabia's Tübingen. The Catholic faculty of theology was absorbed into the ancient University of Tübingen in 1817 and the founder and inspirer was Johann Sebastian von Drey. In writing on inspiration, Drey insisted that the action of the Holy Spirit does not suspend the use of a writer's faculties; it brings a fresh viewpoint, a new outlook. Revelation is a gradual development. The Spirit was at work among the apostles in the primitive Church and 'the faithful preservation of the apostolic writings is the work of the Spirit of God acknowledging his own products' (J.T. Burtchaell, *Catholic Theories of Biblical Inspiration since 1810,* C.U.P. 1961, p. 14). Scripture is a product of the Church, an alternative form of apostolic preaching.

Johann Adam Möhler, a pupil of Drey, wrote that Scripture is the embodiment of tradition. The Church is anterior to Scripture and is founded on the Spirit, not on Scripture. Franz Anton Studenmaier continued in this line. Scripture is written tradition and is fully human and divine. He tended to limit the inspiration of Scripture because certain matters in it did not pertain to dogma. Others of this school set the Bible in the general scheme of the Christian's dependence on the Church. James T. Burtchaell sums up the Tübingen approach very well under four headings (p. 40):

(a) The consigning to writing of revelation, the writing of the Bible, was but one of the functions of the preaching office of prophets and apostles.

(b) The divine charism of grace left the faculties of the writer completely intact. The result is a human-divine writing.

(c) God acts before men's eyes, and man, contemplating his history under grace, comes gradually to a knowledge of God and what he is. The primary medium of revelation is salvation-history.

(d) The Bible is fully human; it is a comparatively undeveloped statement of the Church's faith. Non-revealed elements either do not distort the Gospel or have been filtered out of it. It is instructive to note how the Tübingen school stressed the development of revelation and saw the origin and inspiration of the Bible, especially the New Testament, as part of the life of the community.

About the middle and during the second half of the century many prominent Roman theologians discussed the problem of inspiration. Among them were such names as Giovanni Perrone, Francesco Patrizi, Carlo Vercellone. But there were others in Rome and elsewhere whose contributions were more lasting and/or more influential. It is to some of these that we now turn.

Cardinal Franzelin

One of the most influential theologians in Rome at the time of the First Vatican Council was John Baptist Franzelin. An Austrian Jesuit, Franzelin had been appointed to a professorship of dogmatic theology at the Gregorian University in 1858, a post which he held until his nomination as cardinal in 1876. Franzelin's book *On Divine Tradition and Scripture,* first edition, appeared only after the prorogation of the Council, but his lithographed notes which in substance became the book were well known from about 1860. In 1869 Franzelin had drawn up a document for the Council's Deputation on

Faith. In his treatment of inspiration he naturally wrote what he had been teaching for some years. The sentence of the Decree on Revelation of Vatican I, that the books of the Bible are sacred and canonical 'because, written under the inspiration of the Holy Spirit, they have God as author and as such have been handed on to the Church', is substantially Franzelin's, but polished and purged of academic redundancies. Franzelin formulated his second thesis as follows: 'The inspiration of the books of Scripture is such that God is their author.' The teaching of the Church, and that of Franzelin, is that Scripture (1) is inspired by God, (2) has God as its author, (3) is the word of God. On Franzelin's advice the Council did not analyse or develop the notion of inspiration. He himself did so in his third thesis. Franzelin contributed much to the statement of the Council on inspiration, but his explanation of the manner in which God is author forms no part of conciliar teaching. It will be found quite inadequate, if not incorrect.

To explain the nature of inspiration Franzelin took as his starting point the human notion of author. What is the minimum required that one may be called the author of a book? It is that he be responsible for the ideas, truths, opinions expressed, and that he should order that they be put in writing. The details of the drafting can be left to a secretary without detriment to the status of the author. The ideas are the formal elements of the book for Franzelin, the words the material elements. God, by the inspiring action of the Holy Spirit, gives the ideas, the entire thought-content of the book. Even those ideas, truths, opinions which the author possesses through his own natural experience, environment and education are in some way evoked again, suggested again by the Spirit. This inspiring influence does not extend to the words in which the ideas are expressed. A simple negative assistance was all that was required to prevent the words not being in accord with the ideas. God then would effect, as it were, inarticulate concepts in the mind of the author, who would then clothe them with his own words and literary forms. In this way Franzelin thought he could preserve both the divine activity and authorship in the formation of the book and the human element of variation in style. Franzelin seemed to think that if man is termed author of a book in the proper sense, then God cannot be regarded as author; he would only be giving his help as a first cause.

Franzelin's system can only be subject to a full critique in the light of other systems which explain inspiration. For the moment we can draw attention to several serious objections. (1) The system presupposes a distinction between articulate and inarticulate thought which has no basis in the framework of modern psychology. Our thought cannot dispense with verbal images. It is all but impossible to conceive of God suggesting ideas without clothing them in some sort of verbal image. The internal word expresses itself in the external. (2) In avoiding any system of verbal dictation, Franzelin accepts an even more rigid 'conceptual' dictation – God dictates all the ideas; he suggests ideas ready-made which the writer expresses in his own words. (3) God and man seem to work not in subordination but in conjuction, side by side, to produce the book. They are two juxtaposed causes. It is difficult to see how the book can be wholly God's or wholly man's.

In justice to Franzelin it must be said that some of his proposals in this famous third thesis have been assumed into Papal documents without, of course, any approval or confirmation of his system.

In *Providentissimus Deus* Leo XIII writes:

He (the Holy Spirit) so stirred and moved them to write by a supernatural power, he so stood by them while they were writing, that they correctly understood, willed to write down faithfully and expressed aptly and with infallible truth all that and

only that which he ordered them to write. Otherwise he would not be the author of the whole of
Sacred Scripture (Dz 3293).

The ideas and much of the phraseology are Franzelin's. The purpose of the statement in the encyclical as
well as in Franzelin was to emphasize that the books of
the Bible from their conception to their consignment to
writing were composed entirely under the constant and
positive influence of the Holy Spirit. The encyclical left
aside the disputed question of verbal inspiration. The
Holy Spirit assisted the writers in their writing in such a
way that what he inspired in them was faithfully and
correctly expressed. Leo XIII does not describe the 'how'
of this co-operation.

Franzelin began from the idea of a human author,
from that which is necessary that a man be the author of
a book. This was then applied to God. The method is
quite legitimate but bears within itself the built-in danger
of fastening a purely human notion on to God and di-
minishing the part of the human writer. Franzelin paid
the minimum attention to the personal activity of the human writers. He even avoided giving them the title of
author. 'If man is called author in the proper sense,' he
wrote, 'this is a very denial that God is author.' Franzelin's notion of instrumentality was also deficient.

The Historical Approach of M.-J. Lagrange

There were theologians and biblicists who thought that a
different approach to the problem would shed more
light. Fr M.-J. Lagrange, O.P. was one. He was the most
outstanding scholar of the Catholic biblical revival of the
late nineteenth and early twentieth centuries and the
founder and first director of the deservedly famous
École Biblique in Jerusalem. Lagrange expounded his
views on inspiration in a series of articles in the *Revue*

Biblique in 1895-96 and in his lectures given at the *Institut Catholique* at Toulouse in 1902 and published in Paris the following year. He deals with inspiration in the third lecture. Lagrange analysed Chapter Two of the third session of the first Vatican Council: 'The Church regards these books as holy and canonical... because, written under the inspiration of the Holy Spirit, they have God as author...' The logic progresses in three steps, to repeat what has been said earlier: (1) there are books written under the breath of the Spirit which, therefore, (2) have God as their author, and for this reason (3) the Church regards them as holy and canonical. Instead of constructing a notion of author according to our own standards and imposing it on God, let us start with the books as they are and with the theological notion of inspiration.

Books do not drop ready-made from heaven. They have a history and are regularly the end-product of painstaking toil. We look to history to see how they were composed, remembering always that this composition took place under the constant direction and inflow of the Holy Spirit. We proceed *a posteriori* and historically. We do not philosophize *a priori* as to how God should inspire the Bible so as to be its author. The people of the Bible who had grown to the belief and conviction that they were the people of God belonged to a particular part of the ancient Near East at a particular period in history. Their world-view, cosmology, cosmography, geography, was that of their epoch and culture, much of it, as we now know, quite incorrect. Many of their religious beliefs and practices were primitive, undeveloped, influenced by the environment of the Near East. Polygamy and blood-vengeance were accepted, the death-penalty was inflicted for the violation of certain religious observances and taboos. Abraham took to himself the slave girl Hagar when his wife Sarai was barren (Gen 16). David had a plurality of wives (2 Sam 3); Solomon had them in large numbers (1 Kings 11). The incident of Judah and Tamar is offensive (Gen 38). Jephthah's vow and the sacrifice of his daughter are barbarous (Jud 11. 28-40). Yet the book that records these events is inspired in all its parts. The creation narrative with its weird cosmology is inspired, as is the narrative of the talking snake and Balaam's loquacious donkey (Num 22-24). John's record of the profound prayer for unity (ch. 17) is inspired, as is the theology of original sin and Christ's unique redemptive work in Romans 5.12-21. Sometimes the biblical writer is recording the religious traditions of his people; sometimes he uses written sources, sometimes oral. Now he theologizes upon his heritage, now he commits to writing the theological reflections of others, editing, arranging, adding, commenting. The ancient writers did not know our system of footnotes and so they present to us two or three different accounts of the same tradition (1 Sam 31 and 2 Sam 1; Gen 12.10-20; 20.1-18; 26.1-14; cf. Ch.4). The impassioned utterances of great prophets centuries apart are grouped together under one great patron, as in the book of Isaiah. The personal experiences of men face to face with God are recorded (Is 6; Jer 1; Ez 1-3) as well as the confrontation of man with God-made-man in glory (Acts 9). We read in Proverbs hundreds of wise saws which are the fruit of life's experience; we read a summary of the five books of Jason of Cyrene which we know as the Second Book of Maccabees (2 Mac 2.23). There are letters highly theological as Ephesians, or deeply personal as Philemon. There is on-going revelation in the Bible from Genesis to Apocalypse. All authors and books are inspired. But not all, and at times precious little, of what a writer records has been revealed to him. Much is of purely human origin. Is the writer teaching us all these details, gory and noble, unsavoury and sublime? No, not all of them. Is he recording them? Of course. It is under the direction of the Holy

Spirit that all is being recorded. It is the history of God leading his chosen people to the fullness of revelation, purifying their religious ideas, elevating their moral concepts (cf. Matt 5-7; 19).

Fr Lagrange has wisely set the books of the Bible in the stream of history and has seen that the immediate object of inspiration is to produce a record, to preserve in writing. Its ultimate object is to teach. Lagrange is in full agreement with St Paul. In 1 Cor 10.1-13, Paul writes of God's salvific action which both saves and punishes. He concludes: 'Now these things happened to them as a warning, but they were written down for our instruction...' The Exodus traditions, their liturgical re-enactment and the theological reflections on them were recorded to teach the people of God. And Paul reminds the Church at Rome that 'whatever was written in former days was written for our instruction, that by steadfastness and by the encouragement of the scriptures we might have hope' (Rom 15.4).

Cardinal Newman

Just over a decade before Lagrange began writing on inspiration, Cardinal Newman had made a contribution. In 1884 Newman published two essays on the inspiration of the Scriptures which were re-issued in a revised form in 1890 in a private edition with the title *Stray Essays*. Newman had been thinking over the problem for some decades and the immediate occasion of his writing was a work of Ernest Renan in which the former Catholic seminarian maintained that the Catholic Church insisted on its members accepting certain scriptural information on matters of fact in defiance of criticism and history. Newman asked: '...to what does the Church oblige us? And what is her warrant for doing so?' It is worth citing his reply in full:

31

The matters which she can oblige us to accept with an internal assent are the matters contained in that Revelation of Truth, written or unwritten, which came to the world from our Lord and His Apostles; and this claim on our faith in her decisions as to the matter of that Revelation rests on her being the divinely appointed representative of the Apostles, and the expounder of their words; so that whatever she categorically delivers about their formal acts, or their writings or their teaching, is an Apostolic deliverance. I repeat, the only sense in which the Church 'insists' on any statement, Biblical or other, the only reason for her so insisting, is that that statement is part of the original Revelation, and therefore must be unconditionally accepted – else, that Revelation is not, as a revelation, accepted at all (*On the Inspiration of Scripture,* edd. J. Derek Holmes & Robert Murray, London, Geoffrey Chapman, 1967, p. 103).

We must believe what is revealed and Scripture contains this revelation. The purpose of Newman's first essay had been 'to state what we really do hold as regards Holy Scripture, and what a Catholic is bound to believe.' Has the Church made any pronouncements about Scripture that demand our assent of faith?

I answer that there are two such dogmas: one relates to the authority of Scripture, the other to its interpretation. As to the authority of Scripture, we hold it to be, in all matters of faith and morals, divinely inspired throughout; as to its interpretation, we hold that the Church is, in faith and morals, the one infallible expounder of that inspired text (*ibid.* pp. 106-7).

Newman then asks in what respect are the books of the Canon inspired. Surely not in every respect, because we would then be bound to believe that the earth stands forever, that heaven is above us, that there are no antipodes. Looking to the Council of Trent and to Vatican I, Newman concludes that they 'specify "faith and moral Conduct" as the drift of that teaching which has the guarantee of inspiration.' This is quite true. But Newman was not correct in interpreting the references to faith and morals as expressing a restriction of inspiration. Normative faith and moral conduct are found in the Scriptures duly recorded under the breath of the Spirit. But other matters are recorded under the same Spirit.

Reflecting that the Councils emphasize the inspiration of Scripture in respect to 'faith and Morals' Newman notes that '...they do not say a word directly as to its inspiration in matters of fact.' Then in a remarkable paragraph, which shows a clear understanding of salvation-history without using the term, he explains:

> ...are we to conclude that the record of facts in Scripture does not come under the guarantee of its inspiration? We are not so to conclude...

Inspiration touches the whole saving narrative.

> Scripture is inspired, not only in faith and morals, but in all its parts which bear on faith, including matters of fact (p. 110).

In his second essay, which was a reply to the Maynooth professor Dr Healy (soon to be a bishop, later Archbishop of Tuam), Newman returns to the total inspiration of Scripture which 'is inspired in its length and breadth... whenever, wherever, and by whomsoever written, it is all inspired...' But, he continues, we may still ask, 'In what respect and for what purpose?' (*ibid.* p. 150).

Newman saw clearly that the purpose of the Bible was religious. It was inspired so as to preserve genuine revelation. He was interested above all in the purpose of inspiration and was of the opinion that the Church had defined inspiration in terms of its relationship to revelation. Inspiration comes fully into play when Scripture is expressing God's revelation. Because he linked inspiration and revelation so closely, Newman could be understood as restricting inspiration to matters of revelation or to faith and morals. One must admit that had he clarified his terminology he would have avoided a number of difficulties and misunderstandings. Unfortunately Newman is remembered in the manuals of theology as a rather dubious quantity who would leave *obiter dicta* outside the scope of inspiration, and hence of inerrancy. Towards the end of his first essay he asked whether *obiter dicta* were conceivable in an inspired document. In papal utterances or in conciliar pronouncements '*obiter dicta*' is the phrase used to describe those parts which are not contained within the scope of the formal definition, and imply no intention of binding the consciences of the faithful. Newman saw no serious difficulty in admitting their existence in Scripture. An example of such *obiter dicta* would be the statement in the Book of Judith that Nebuchadnezzar was king of Nineveh. Newman had quoted a passage from Professor Lamy, who would not accept such *obiter dicta* in Scripture and who cited as alleged examples of such what is said of Tobias' dog and the cloak which Paul left at Troas. This is the origin of Newman's name being associated with these two episodes in the manuals of theology. Newman did not associate *obiter dicta* with error or falsehood. He explained in his second essay that he meant by *obiter dicta* 'phrases, clauses or sentences in Scripture about matters of mere fact, which, as not relating to faith or morals, may without violence be referred to the human element in its composition,' and again '... a phrase or sentence which, whether a statement of literal fact or not, is not from the circumstances binding on our faith' (pp. 141-2). In the final analysis it would matter little if Paul had made a mistake in his second letter to Timothy. If he had left his cloak with Eutychus and not, as he said, with Carpus, this would scarcely shake our confidence in the profound theology of the letters to the churches at Rome and Ephesus.

It would not be accurate to say that Newman anticipated fully Vatican II, that he proposed precisely what this Council proposes. But he was clearly moving towards the position which the Council states, namely that the Scriptures propound faithfully, firmly, without error that truth which God has consigned to them for our salvation. Newman understood the *purpose* of inspiration to be the consignment of revelation to writing for our instruction and salvation. The purpose of inspiration then was not to preserve statements about what did not pertain to revelation. Hence Paul's cloak left at Troas, Tobias' dog trotting behind him, would not fall under inspiration/revelation because such episodes had no connection with revelation or our salvation. Yet Newman did maintain that the breath of the Spirit, inspiration, touched the whole Bible. Vatican II has vindicated in substance what Newman was trying to say. Strictly speaking Newman could be accused of contradicting himself, or at least of inconsistency.

For more than twenty years after Lagrange's contribution the study of inspiration remained stagnant. This was in large part due to the Modernist crisis in the first decade of the century and the very severe reaction to it in official Church documents. At the same time the Pontifical Biblical Commission maintained a very negative attitude to modern advances in biblical studies, though its heavily loaded decrees almost left the door sufficiently open for an adroit exegete to wriggle his way through. The manuals of theology generally speaking repeat the teaching of Vatican I, quote the encyclicals of Leo XIII, Benedict XV and Pius XII and give a brief but suspicious nod to the progress made in biblical studies since the turn of the century. They are pre-occupied with defending the inerrancy of Scripture and with proving that God is the author of Scripture. (In this sweeping generalization exception must be made for Christian Pesch's masterly work *On the Inspiration of Sacred Scripture,* 1906.) There is little of the historical approach and the discussions are apologetic and polemical in tone.

Pierre Benoit

For more than twenty years Pierre Benoit of the *École Biblique* of Jerusalem has been contributing to the discussion of inspiration. His first contribution was a translation of and commentary on St Thomas' *Summa* 2a 2ae, qq. 171-178. Benoit has constantly warned that St Thomas did not envisage our present-day problems and that he did not use the word 'inspiration' precisely as we use it today. St Thomas discussed inspiration in the context of prophecy and has a basically intellectual concept of both inspiration and revelation. Inspiration was the elevation of the mind, revelation was the perception of divine things. The prophet in the light of the Spirit elevating his mind saw the divine truth and handed it on. St Thomas did not discuss scriptural inspiration as we understand it.

Benoit looks to man's speculative and practical judgments. The speculative judgment is theoretical; it has as its object the true; the practical judgment looks to the good. Both these judgments share in the divine impulse of inspiration. It is the prophet in whom the speculative judgment is more at work, the sacred writer whose practical judgment is to the fore. The prophet has truth revealed to him, truth at which he could not arrive unaided. The hagiographer, using the word in the broadest sense of one who writes under God's direction, sees that something is good, something is to be written. What and how he will write will depend on his purpose. He will write naturally in those forms which are part of his cultural heritage and which he bends, bursts or forges as he struggles to give utterance to his experience. Benoit called the process in which the speculative judgment was primarily concerned 'prophetic inspiration', that in which the practical judgment was predominant 'scriptural.' The terminology led to a misunderstanding, as some feared that Benoit was denying to the prophet any impulse that might extend to writing, and to the sacred writer any illumination of this knowledge or revelation of supernatural truths. But Benoit had never done this. He saw clearly that, depending on the matter and circumstances, now the speculative judgment, now the practical judgment would be more involved. But he acknowledged the difficulty of the terminology. To avoid the impression that prophetic inspiration may be a different charism from scriptural inspiration, i.e. that there must be a dichotomy between the two, he proposed what he recognized as a not very elegant term, 'cognitive' inspiration. This cognitive inspiration is 'a light which illuminates the speculative judgment and raises it to a supernatural mode of knowledge'. Inerrancy is involved only when the speculative judgment operates, when there is the affirmation 'this is true', in short when the writer is teaching. The difficulty of course is to decide when the writer is teaching and when he is merely recording. Is he affirming a truth which he has worked out under the guidance of the Spirit? Is he merely speaking, quoting, with no affirmation? Is he giving but a qualified affirmation? There could be the danger of understanding the writer as speaking merely in propositions and of justifying each statement according to its degree of affirmation or of teaching.

This approach is very academic and abstract, and Benoit is aware of it. He does not want to remove scriptural inspiration from the context of inspiration in general, that is, from the context of the general action of the Holy Spirit. There is but one Holy Spirit active in both the Old and New Testaments. Before the Spirit moved men to write, he moved them to speak; before he moved them to speak, he moved them to act. The Scriptures record the deeds of men who helped form a nation, a people, a church. They record what men said in this formative process. In the course of the years and the centuries men and groups reflected on history and experience under the light of the Spirit. Benoit suggests that the term 'biblical inspiration' in the broad sense cover this whole area. Biblical inspiration will be:

cognitive – an illumination of the understanding,

oratorical – a practical impulse to speak or compose a discourse,

scriptural – a practical impulse to write down, to compose a book.

This division looks primarily to the *source* of inspiration, to the Spirit as it first touches the spirit of man. In its *effect,* then, biblical inspiration will be dramatic, prophetic-apostolic, hagiographical according as the Spirit moves man to communicate the divine message by his concrete life, by his words or by his writings. These divisions are not watertight compartments. They flow into one another and blend in different ways.

God inspires in order to reveal truth, which is himself. '...He inspires pastors, orators, and writers, who having perceived this truth pass it on, by living it, by speaking it, and by committing it to writing' (*Inspiration and the Bible*, Sheed & Ward, 1965, p. 46). The Bible is the end-product of much human activity under the Spirit and has demanded active participation by the charismatic. When he eventually speaks or writes, he does so within the limits of human language which certainly conveys the truth, but in a very limited way. He does not speak in revealed propositions. Every sentence is not to be put to the critical test of inerrancy. The sacred author is one who passes on revelation because he has experienced God:

...Revelation appears as a broad, many-faceted

and analogical charism involved in all supernatural teaching of divine truth. All the sacred authors benefit by it, each in his own way. Whether this be under the impulse of an imaginative or sensible vision sent by God or by an intellectual illumination bringing to the mind new ideas adapted to the divine mystery, or whether it be in simple meditation on the human experience of everyday life, in each case the mind of God's elect is elevated, strengthened and enlightened by a supernatural light which makes it more efficacious and enables it to draw from infused or acquired data the supernatural doctrine that God has destined for his people. This teaching will not be expressed in every sentence the sacred author writes. Indeed, the greater part of what he writes will not be revelation in the strict sense at all. But the idea, the judgment, the doctrine, that God wishes to convey will emerge from a thousand phrases of minimal importance. And it is this that merits their being considered revelation in the broad sense (*ibid*. p. 15).

As Benoit so rightly says, it is important to connect 'scriptural' inspiration with its antecedents and to retain its historical setting.

To isolate the inspiration of the Bible from its inspired preparation in Action and Word is to run the risk of sterilizing the Bible by rectifying it, to make it as barren as an abstract textbook, a collection of terse, private 'truths' which, torn from the soil that nourished them, can only deceive (*Concilium* 1, Dec. 1965, p. 8).

A final and important contribution of Benoit's is his linking of inspiration and revelation in the overall view of the Bible. 'Revelation is the immediate corollary of inspiration, its end and effect, a different aspect of, but connected with, the same charism' (*ibid*. p. 10). At times biblical revelation flows from the intense activity of the human mind raised by Spirit; at times it is the result of long grappling with human problems under the Spirit:

> Everything in the Bible is inspired, but not everything is revealed. Or, to be more precise, the entire work builds up to a full revelation which disengages itself from the whole; but each detail, though it be inspired, does not contain in addition a revelation commanding the assent of faith (*ibid.* p. 12).

Karl Rahner

Karl Rahner sets inspiration in the foundation of the Church. He does not proceed historically. He does not take the Bible itself as his starting point but rather the doctrine of inspiration as established by the teaching authority of the Church and explained and expounded by the theologians. He comments that this notion is rather abstract and must be given material content. Rahner looks for an activity of God which will make him literary author of the Bible while at the same time not merely tolerating but positively demanding human authorship. He says that inspiration consists in

> ...God's supernaturally enlightening the human author's mind in the perception of the content and essential plan of the book, and moving his will to write no more and no less than what God himself wants written, God providing him the while with special assistance to ensure that the work, thus conceived and willed, be correspondingly carried into effect (*Studies in Biblical Theology,* Burns & Oates, 1965, p. 13).

This is very much the description given by Leo XIII in *Providentissimus Deus.* Rahner will have God as the literary author without attributing to him the literary form of the book or section of the book. To illustrate his thought he takes as an example the letter to Philemon of which God is the author although he did not write it:

> ...his authorship consists precisely in his absolute and efficacious will that the Church, as a community of love, should manifest for all ages 'canonically' her nature, her faith, and her love, even in such a letter. Because God wills the letter in this fashion, which is not the way of human action, though for this very reason it must involve human activity, the particular literary genre of the writing will not have the effect of specifying God's authorship (*ibid*. p. 82).

Rahner distinguished clearly literary originator (*Urheber*) and author in the literary sense *(Verfasser)*. With equal clarity he describes God as literary author, but in an analogous sense, such that the divine authorship is distinguished from the human authorship. Rahner's general thesis is that God founds (1) the Church, (2) the apostolic Church, (3) with Scripture as a constitutive element.

1) God wills the Church absolutely, by a formal predefinition, in the context of salvation-history. The design for the incarnation of the Logos includes within it the foundation of the Church. The work of salvation-history is God's in a higher way than the works of nature. In the latter God acts upon the historical world, in the former he enacts his own history within the world. The qualitatively unique climax of the historical action of God is in Christ and the Church. This divine act is eschatological. So in the foundation of the Church we have (i) God's formal predefinition, (ii) the setting of salvation-history, (iii) an eschatological event.

2) The apostolic Church is in many ways unique. What comes later rests upon what was earlier. The foundation of the Church was Christ and the apostolic community. God had a unique relationship to the first gener-

41

ation of the Church, such a relationship as is not transmissible, precisely because he is the founder of the Church. The relationship which he has to other periods of the Church he has through the apostolic Church. The beginning, the being-born, has something unique about it. In the apostolic Church revelation is still being given, not merely being handed on. One distinguishes coming into existence and continuing in existence. And the Church *in fieri,* coming into existence, has God as 'author' in a special way.

3) The Bible belongs to the constitutive elements of this apostolic Church which was the qualitatively unique work of God and the permanent 'canonical' origin of the later Church. The oral *paradosis,* that which was to be passed on, enjoyed priority within the apostolic Church. It possessed both authority and infallibility. The apostolic Church reduced to writing her *paradosis,* her faith. The Bible is the Church's self-expression of her faith. Rahner can now formulate his thesis:

> ...*by the fact that* God wills and creates the apostolic Church with a formal predefinition that is within salvation-history and eschatological in character, and thereby so wills and creates her constitutive elements, God wills and creates the Scriptures in such a way as to become through his inspiration their originator, their author (*ibid.* pp. 52-3).

The inspiration of Scripture then 'is nothing else then God's founding of the Church in as much as this applies precisely to that constitutive element of the apostolic Church which is the Bible' (*ibid.* p. 53).

The Scriptures are in their origin just as much the expression of the fact of the primitive Church as they are the word of God. They are the written embodiment of what she believed and of what, believing, she laid down for herself. To deny this would be to deny that the writers were true authors and to reduce them to a state of mere transmitters of the message from above. The writings of the New Testament have their origin in the life process of the Church. Rahner must now account for the Old Testament. He does so in this manner. Firstly we must remember that inspiration and canonicity are conceptually and in fact two different things. But they are not entirely independent. Inspiration is only fully there, that is, fully manifested and known as such, when acknowledged. God does not write or cause to have written a book for itself. The book is only fully meaningful when it 'arrives' and is recognized with utter certainty as God's. For the Old Testament the synagogue had no infallible teaching authority. There were prophets, but no infallible Church. The synagogue could fall away from God. There were certainly at that time writings that were acknowledged as canonical and inspired; but this knowledge of the Old Testament canonicity and inspiration was confirmed by Christ, the apostles and the Church. Because of prophecy, knowledge of inspiration and canonicity could begin. But the Church did not take over a ready-made canon.

The whole process of formation of the Old Testament, continues Rahner, was completed only in the New. Hence it follows that the writings of the Old Testament were ultimately planned by God in so far as they were to have and preserve their validity and function in the New Testament. The Old Testament is not merely a *de facto* account of the pre-history of the Church and of man's path to the fulness of truth. It was designed to be such, for its own very search could only be completed in the New Testament. The Old Testament is the authentic crystallization of the Church's pre-history, of God's dealings with man, of man-in-Israel's experience of God. In so far then as God causes the Old Testament as the definitive image of the pre-history of the Church, of her experience with God and of God's dealing with her, he inspires the Scriptures and makes them his own as author.

Yves Congar agrees substantially with Rahner. He sees the author as 'he who has the responsibility for something, since he is there at the very source and origin.' Congar would be more specific as to the formal and proper subject of inspiration. To say that Scripture is a written expression of the faith of the primitive Church is correct, but of itself insufficient. The Church was conscious not only of possessing the Scriptures as a written fixation of her faith; she was conscious of having received them from men chosen by God – the apostles. It is Rahner's expression rather than content that Congar would polish. The authority of the apostles *in* the Church can be seen as Rahner presents his thesis; their authority *over* the Church is less clear. The proper subject of inspiration is not a shapeless mass, the primitive Church. It is properly the prophets and the apostles.

Social Inspiration

John McKenzie followed the lead given by Karl Rahner and wrote of the social character of inspiration. Inspiration is supernatural and the only aspect of it that is open to historical and critical investigation is the literary activity of the inspired authors and the growth of the book. In expounding McKenzie's approach I will intersperse some comments which I hope will not obscure or distort his genuine insights. *The Encyclopaedia Britannica* and *David Copperfield* are books, but of quite different kinds. Were one to remove the sub-titles, names of authors, etc. from the *Britannica,* would one have something like the Bible? Were the biblical books compilations? Yes and no. Many of the books of the Old Testament had a long history. Genesis and Exodus have woven together, at times inextricably, the Yahwistic, Elohistic and Priestly narratives, each having its origin and development in different circles in different places. Within each tradition there were stories in varied oral forms grouped around names personal and local. There were oral traditions for the songs and laws of the Old Testament. Man spoke before he wrote. Writing in the ancient world was a record of what was spoken, an aid to memory. As the tradition was handed down either in writing or orally there was freedom of interpretation. As each balladist sang or narrated he 'created' anew. No-one thinks, McKenzie remarks, that the terminal editor is the only inspired author. I would suggest that Benoit's distinction between prophetic and scriptural inspiration may be of use here. Perhaps it is that the terminal editor is the only 'scripturally' inspired author. The Spirit, who is always one and the same, works in all, moving men to act, speak, record, interpret. But it was only the final editor, redactor, theologian, author who was ultimately moved to write this and that, in this way, in this order and form. He was the 'scripturally' inspired author.

Supposing that the Yahwist is the first great literary creator of ancient Israel. McKenzie asks if he is the only inspired contributor in respect of the matter he controls, orders, interprets. Others, he says, had a share that was clearly more than nothing. I suggest that the Yahwist is the scripturally inspired author. The others share in the charism short of presenting the matter in its definitive form. The *Logia* (collections of the sayings) and accounts of the deeds of Jesus received their form in the Christian apostolic community. There was catechesis, question and answer. Jesus' sayings were adapted and applied and interpreted into the life-situation of each church. They received some written form and finally the definitive written form and gospel-setting in which we now have them. Obviously many people contributed. Do all who contributed creatively share in inspiration? In prophetic inspiration, yes; in scriptural inspiration...? Or is it too mechanical to distribute inspiration among those who have in some way, however remotely, contributed to the book? We must remember that it is the same Spirit working in the individual as in the community, in the Old Testament as in the New. We must remember too that the final author-redactor-editor would have left much of his material untouched. His additions here and there, his modifications and adaptations would often give the book or passage a different direction. Scriptural inspiration is at its fullest when the book receives its final form and is accepted as part of Scripture. It seems then that we must distribute scriptural inspiration over many contributors and in different degrees.

When we speak of instrumental cause, continues McKenzie, we are in difficulties. Quite often, it is the rule for the Old Testament, we know neither the author nor the extent of any single person's contribution, which must remain for the most part quite undefined. But there is a difference. The contribution of Paul to Galatians, Romans, 1 & 2 Corinthians is clear; Luke's contribution to Luke-Acts is somewhat different, but still clear. The position of the gospels is different still. And most of the books of the Old Testament demand a number of authors. McKenzie therefore looks for a principle of unity in the formation of the literature which will make the charism more intelligible. He looks to the social character of inspiration. The charism is in the Church. Those who write do so as officers of the Church. God is using his community, both in the Old and New Testaments, to produce a book. I would ask, then, are there not so much degrees of inspiration as different levels at which the members of a community share a charism which is directed to the production of a book?

Much of the literature of the ancient Near East is anonymous. McKenzie asks if the ancient author saw himself as a spokesman of society and considered society the real author of literature? He was recording the traditions and beliefs of a people. This, I think, needs not a little qualification. In the first chapter of Genesis, for example, we have a very theological and quite sophisticated reflection on the relationship between God and the universe, between God and man. In ch. 3, to which ch. 2 is a necessary lead-up, we read the story of Israel's everyman, the result of profound reflection on the experience that man is divided in himself, from his fellow man, that he must sweat and toil for his livelihood. But it is scarcely the 'belief of a people'. It became so later when accepted. And look at the barbarous and idolatrous conduct of the people in the narratives of Samuel-Kings. The author is judging both kings and people against the standards demanded by the law of the covenant.

What is the identifying and unifying trait of biblical literature? McKenzie asks. It is '...a recital of the saving acts of God, a profession of the faith of Israel and of the primitive Church.' The author, then, wishes to be the voice of Israel, the voice of the Church. He did not wish to express his own individuality. But here we must call 'Halt.' Was Job the voice of Israel? Was not the traditional theology of Israel quite unsatisfactory for him? He well may be the voice of the true Israel, but it is only much later that we know this. In what sense is the author-redactor of the Song of Songs the voice of Israel? And surely Qohelet and Paul expressed their individuality and wanted to do so. The writer writes what his society communicates to him, certainly. But that is only part of the story. Society and the elders of Israel formed the non-liturgical laws. These were accepted and written down. But there is much theologizing, e.g. from the Deuteronomistic historian; there is re-interpretation and re-application, as in the prophetic literature, and there is much sheer assembling, as in the hundreds of wise sayings in the Writings.

For the prophet the word of God is an experience of the reality of God. When he utters the word, he responds to this experience. The experience is a movement to speak or write the word of God. This the prophet does in the context of the faith, experience and traditions of his people. If this seems to identify inspiration and revelation, then McKenzie is ready to plead guilty. 'Inspiration has been too closely identified with the individual author and with the written word; revelation has been too simply understood as a revealed proposition, and not as the word of God and the knowledge of God in the biblical sense' (*Myths and Realities: Studies in Biblical Theology,* Bruce, 1963, pp. 67-8).

The vehicle of inspiration is the community of the people of God, Israel and the Church. There are degrees of revelation in both Old and New Testaments. The letters of Jude and the second and third letters of John are not as valuable as the gospels or Paul's letters. Genesis and Isaiah are more theologically significant than Chronicles and Maccabees. All books are the word of God but some are 'less inspired in the sense that the clarity of insight and the vigor of personal response is less in some men than in others' (*ibid.* p. 69).

McKenzie's insight, sparked by Rahner, that inspiration must be set in the community is valid. This insight has been modified and developed by Dennis McCarthy. Recognizing rightly that the Bible was formed in, by and for a society, he saw it an oversimplification 'to take as absolute the statement that the ancient author was in all instances the spokesman of society, and society was the real author of his book' (*Theological Studies* 24 [1963] p. 553). The ancient lost himself in society in a way that is strange to us, and ancient literature was a product and part of tradition; beliefs, forms of expression were maintained and passed on in a degree beyond what we know. The individual worked under the pressure of tradition. The two played their part, society and individual.

We must be careful, McCarthy continues, not to equate mysticism and inspiration. The experiences of Isaiah, Jeremiah, Ezechiel are not inspiration. Inspiration is the impulse to write. There is much theologizing on history in the Old Testament, that is, reflection on historical experience in the light of revealed notions. The Yahwistic document, for example, is

> a brilliant response to the question posed by the organization and expansion of Israel under David. The secure possession of the land flowing with milk and honey is seen as the term of a divinely directed historical process, the concrete evidence of the favour of Yahweh (*ibid*. pp. 558-9).

The Yahwist's experience of the divine was not mystical. It came in and through the experience of the historical situation reflected upon in the light of his beliefs. The experience of Dt 6-28 was the opposite of that of the Yahwist. The author saw the threatened loss of the land. A featureless anonymity did not shape Deuteronomy. One can ask, were the stories behind the material inspired, e.g. the stories behind Gen 2-3, the official archives that were the basis of the history of the kings of Israel? I would not think so. These were at the disposal of the writers either as part of his cultural heritage or as state documents. The writers used them for a purpose and in this use the charism of inspiration came into play. The writer was certainly at the service of the community. He selected what served the life of the community. McCarthy continues:

> Just as he had used traditional materials, reworked them and marked them by his own experience and reflection, so he knew his own work would become part of tradition to be used (*ibid*. p. 561).

Why write? To communicate, to preserve. The writer will communicate something to future generations, to build up the people of God. But some individual had to do the work of writing, ordering. The interaction of society and individual, believing community and believing member, tradition and individual genius must be balanced.

49

These modern theologians and exegetes whose contributions we have just discussed have given the theology of inspiration a desperately needed stimulus. Our gain from their struggle with the problem may be summed up roughly as follows:

1) Inspiration must be set in the life of the people of God and in the life of the Church. The Tübingen theologians of the first half of the last century had seen this.

2) Inspiration must be seen in the context of the action of the one and same Spirit who moves men to act, to speak, to write.

3) It is most advantageous to proceed historically, from the formation of the books as we know them.

4) We must consider the action and inter-action of community and individual in the formation of the Bible.

5) The purpose of biblical inspiration is to preserve in writing a gradually developing and unfolding revelation. This comes through reflection in faith and under the Spirit on history and tradition.

CHAPTER 3

INSPIRATION IN THE FORMATION OF THE BOOKS OF THE BIBLE

Many explanations of inspiration both in ecclesiastical documents and in the writings of theologians had been characterized by two tendencies: (1) to proceed *a priori,* that is to analyse the notion of author and to ask what would be the conditions necessary so that God could be justly given this title, (2) to speak as if there were one author for each book. And the contemporary theology of revelation had been rather constricting. God had often been presented as if he were revealing himself in propositions. Despite all this the First Vatican Council has given us the clue as to what should be the most fruitful starting point in the study of inspiration. As we have seen the Council stated that the books of the Bible were (1) written *(conscripti),* (2) under the Spirit, (3) and so have God as author. We should proceed from the writing of the books. This is what Fr Lagrange did and we shall follow him. From their complicated process of growth we shall see how difficult it is to describe inspiration and how inadequate it is in general to describe it as if each book had a single author.

The Making of the Books of the Bible

1) *Old Testament:*
a) *The 'Histories':* We do not know the authors of most of the books of the Bible. Until about a century ago it was thought Moses wrote the Petateuch, David most of the Psalms, solomon much of the Wisdom Literature. But scholarship has shown that many of the Old Testament books were centuries in the making. These books in fact would have had countless 'authors'. The

book of Judges, for example, has had a long history. The raw material of the book goes back to the twelfth century B.C., to the exploits of tribal heroes and the oral traditions about them which were in circulation among the various tribes. In the period of the two Kingdoms, about 925-721 B.C., two collections were made of these traditions, one in the north and one in the south. After the fall of Samaria and the destruction of the Northern Kingdom in 721 B.C. the two collections were united by another editor with a moralizing introduction. Later the Deuteronomic author edited the work again, stressing the religious lessons. Probably about the fifth century the work was given the form in which we know it with the addition of the minor judges and the appendices, namely the sanctuaries of Micah and of Dan and the crime at Gibeah and the war against Benjamin. The book was 800 years in the making. In his introduction to the French fasicule of Judges in the Jerusalem Bible Abbé Vincent of Strasbourg concludes:

> The book is not the work of a single author. It is the work of an inspired tradition which produced a growth in revelation by directing the successive redactors to give us the important lesson of loyalty to God.

An inspired tradition may seem to us to be a little vague. Perhaps it is, but we must be content with it. The Spirit of God worked in the people of God and in certain individuals; few or many, and we shall never know who they were, contributed in a special way to make the book what it now is.

The book of Deuteronomy has an interesting history. It is a widely accepted hypothesis that the original Deuteronomy, the book found in the Temple (2 Kings 22.3ff.), consisted of the body of law (ch. 12-26), the introduction immediately preceding it (ch. 5-11), and ch. 28. The whole corpus from Deuteronomy through to the end of the second book of Kings, in the form in which we now possess it, is the work of one who is commonly known as the Deuteronomic historian. He wrote the history of Israel from Moses to the release of King Jehoiachin in exile about 561 B.C. It is the general opinion that the work was composed by one man who wanted to present a theological interpretation of the catastrophes of the destruction of Israel in 721 and of Judah in 587. (Some scholars do not accept the hypothesis of a single author or redactor of Deuteronomy-Kings especially, and this is but one reason, because of the very slight Deuteronomic influence in the books of Samuel. Judges has certainly been subject to Deuteronomistic *editing*; 1-2 Kings were *composed* by the Deuteronomist; cf. Sellin-Fohrer, *Introduction to the Old Testament,* N.Y., Abingdon Press, 1968, pp. 192-5. But this does not affect the point being made here, namely the multiplicity of sources, authors, redactors in the formation of the books.) The work is aimed at showing that the tragedy of Israel was the immediate consequence of apostasy and the persistent failure to obey the divine requirements (2 Kings 17.7ff.). The author had many sources before him and he refers to them constantly, e.g. 2 Kings 21.17. He picked and chose carefully, he edited, he incorporated sagas and traditions often, it seems, without any alteration. As the historians of the ancient Middle East did not have our system of footnotes, they often set side by side different accounts of the same event, e.g. the two accounts of the death of Saul in 1 Sam 21 and 2 Sam 1 and the different versions of the rise of the monarchy interwoven in 1 Sam 8-12. He overlaid all this with his theological interpretation and prefaced the whole with the Deuteronomic law which he set in an immediate line with Moses and hence with the will of God.

b) *Genesis and 'the Fall':*
The final redactor-author of the Creation-Fall narra-

tive of Genesis 2-3 is himself a theologian and the heir of a great theological tradition. His experience is that man is divided in himself, is divided from his fellow; that family is divided against family, nation against nation. The traditions and history of his people tell the same story. How did this come about? The religious thinkers of the tradition believe in a good provident God who did not cause this situation. So it must have had its origin in man, in the powers of evil which are personified by the snake, the symbol of Canaanite fertility cult and of ancient wisdom and magic, all of which had continually turned the Israelites from their convenant obligations to Yahweh. So, reflects the writer, ever since man has been man this is what he has done. It is the story of Everyman. And three times the pattern is repeated in the stories of Cain, the Deluge and the Tower of Babel as man tries to live a law to himself independent of God. Each time disaster follows. And in this long theological tradition within the people of God the Holy Spirit is at work. He is at work too in that long tradition of religious reflection, that quasi-liturgical recitative which we know as the Priestly creation account, Gen. 1.1-2. 4a.

The Holy Spirit has moved men to record for us their struggles with the problems of life, with the problem of an all-good God and evil, with the problem of a people chosen and given a promise yet all but destroyed. In these experiences of life, in these reflections on history and tradition, all steeped in faith and a belief in a one true God, they confront God and gradually ever so slowly, see some facet of what he is, of this fidelity to man whom he has made, to a people whom he has chosen. The purpose of 'inspiration' is to record this experience of, this groping for, God as men reflect on their history and their personal and social life. Its purpose is to record revelation, not in the form of conciliar propositions and neat formulas, but as human experiences of God in life under the Spirit.

c) *Wisdom in Israel:*

Wisdom literature had a long and widespread tradition in the ancient Near East from Mesopotamia across to Egypt. Israel's wisdom-writers lived in, inherited this tradition and made their own peculiar contribution, though at times it may be difficult to see it. One needs no light from the Spirit to know that:

> It is better to live in a desert, than with a garrulous and testy woman (Prov 21.19).

> As a jewel of gold in a pig's snout, so is a beautiful woman without discretion (Prov 11.22).

And so on through the hundreds of wise saws of the book of Proverbs. The Israelite, the Semite, did not distinguish nature and super-nature. All was a unity. And his wise saws are the fruit of his experience in the world that God has made. That old cynic Qoheleth (Ecclesiastes) reflects on the impossibility of understanding what God has done. This is *the* theme of the book. And he reflects on and discards as insufficient many of the wise proverbs which are meant to help man deal with the mystery of God's action. We see just how far a certain person, with a certain character and mentality, in a definite locality and at a definite time in the history of salvation, can advance in solving his problems with a religious tradition and a deficient light which was not the fulness of revelation. The Spirit at work in the people has had this committed to writing for our instruction.

The people of God worshipped at the Temple. They sang the praises of Yahweh and recalled his saving deeds. At times they lamented over national or personal disasters. At times they simply cried out in reverence before the one true God. They adopted forms of speech of the surrounding cultures and even adapted whole Psalms from them, e.g. Ps 29. In the 150 Psalms of the Bible we have a record of the liturgical life of Israel for a period of six or seven hundred years, from the time of David down to the fourth century. The Psalms have been reedited, added to, rehearsed continually in the Temple liturgy. The spirit has preserved for us the prayer life of the people of God which was to become the Church of God.

d) *The Prophets:*
As the people of Israel, leaders, priests and citizens diverged from the law of God under the influence of Canaanite culture, prophets arose to call them back to their duty to God. Amos spoke in the Nothern Kingdom in the days of Uzziah, King of Judah 783-742, and Jeroboam, king of Israel 786-746. He was moved by the Spirit to speak out and to castigate. We have no record that he wrote. His oracles were collected and finally edited, it seems, in Judaean circles – note the precedence given to the King of Judah over the King of Israel – and then circulated. Hosea spoke in the north about the middle of the eighth century and his oracles were gathered together according to some loose system of catch-words or themes. The prophetic book under the name of Isaiah extends over more than two centuries. Most of ch. 1-12 come from the great prophet Isaiah of the eighth century who confronted Ahaz and Hezekiah. Some of ch. 17-23 and most of ch. 28-32 are also from him. The oracles against the nations ch. 13-16 are later and of uncertain date as are ch. 33-4. And ch. 24-7, the Apocalypse of Isaiah, are quite late, from the fifth or fourth century. The whole of ch. 40-55 is late exilic, while ch. 56-66 show many signs of the post-exilic period and the years immediately preceding or following the dedication of the second Temple in 515 B.C. There is a continuous ongoing re-editing, re-interpretation and adaptation. The prophet Jeremiah was active 626-587 B.C. He was moved by the Spirit to act symbolically, to speak out, to dictate his thoughts to his scribe. The events of his life and many of his oracles were later put together in an order that is not always easy to follow. The oracles of

some of the prophets were scattered over just a few years, five or six, and were later gathered together, e.g. Haggai and Zechariah ch. 1-8, who spoke in the years immediately preceding the dedication of the second Temple. The prophets were under the Spirit, and those who recorded, edited, adapted their oracles did so under the same Spirit.

2) *The New Testament:*

As Jesus was founding his Church it was the Spirit that worked in him (cf. Matt 3.16;4.1; Luke 4.18-20). The Spirit came upon him at the baptism, drove him into the desert, was with him when he preached in the synagogue at Capernaum. It was the Spirit that moved the apostles to throw in their lot with him. After the events of the Passion, Resurrection, Ascension and the Pentecost it was again the Spirit that moved the apostles and disciples to act and to speak. It was the Spirit that continually moved and inspired Paul in his missionary journeys. The book of the Acts may well be called the book of the Holy Spirit. It was the Spirit that formed the primitive Church moving the apostles and the Christians to act and speak in furthering God's Kingdom in the process of salvation-history.

The Spirit was in the whole Church, but especially in those men who were charged with its formation and development. Within twenty years of the first Pentecost Paul, the convert Pharisee who was steeped in Jewish tradition, was dictating his letters to the infant churches. He was trying to express for the first time in Greek, his second language, the mystery of salvation. In the letters to the churches in Galatia and in Rome we experience with him all the effort as he labours to express in human language what is ultimately incapable of exhaustive or even at times of adequate expression. His language shows all that strain and stress as does the language of Thucydides when he pioneered a philosophy of history in the opening chapters of his *Peloponnesian War*. Paul drew on all his knowledge of Hebrew religion and observance learned at Jerusalem under Gamaliel, on his experience with the Risen Lord on the road to Damascus, his experience on his missionary ventures and his confrontation with the fervent converts from Judaism to Christianity. And there was his own rich and dynamic personality. The Spirit worked in him as he wrote, that same Spirit that had already inspired him to act, to journey, to speak and instruct. At times the Spirit moved him to write. It was then that he was scripturally inspired.

As the apostles and disciples moved further from Jerusalem and more non-Jews submitted through the kerygma to the glorified Jesus, questions were asked about the person of this Jesus. What did he say? What did he do? How do his words and deeds apply to our community, solve our problems? It was then that the disciples went back to the words, miracles and discussions of Jesus. When Jesus walked Palestine there was no one to accompany him with a tape-recorder. There were no correspondents from the *Nazareth News* or the *Olivet Courier* to report verbatim next day his homily in the synagogue or his passages of arms with the leaders of the Jews. The disciples naturally remembered what he said and did. And now, looking back through the incomparable experience of the first Easter and Pentecost, they related what he had said and done. They selected from the stories and sayings that were to hand, applied and adapted them to the needs and problems of the communities. Groups of stories and sayings were collected and put together so that the communities might know Jesus in action; some of his aphorisms and pronouncements were arranged in an order and by these the new Christians could direct their lives. The Spirit worked in the Apostolic preachers as they told of Jesus' sayings and deeds, the Spirit worked in the communities as they posed questions about Jesus. The Spirit was at work in a special way as certain men, apostles or under apostolic aegis, committed to writing their accounts of what Jesus was.

Many people shared in the charism of inspiration in varying degrees in the formation of the gospels. As Luke tells us, many had undertaken to compile a narrative of what Jesus had said and done, taking their material from eye-witnesses and ministers of the word. Now he himself was taking pains to assemble a clear and connected account of these events 'that you may know the truth concerning the things of which you have been informed' (Lk 1.1-4). Many contributed to the gospel of Matthew. There were those who collected Logia and stories, those who applied and adapted the discourses and parables of Jesus, and the no mean theologian and convert from Judaism who fashioned the deeply theological first two chapters. And the final editor-author who arranged the five discourses with the recurring ending: 'And when Jesus finished these saying...' enjoyed the charism of scriptural inspiration, the inspiration to write and communicate saving truth. But more of this in Chapter Five.

Individual and Community

It has been said that the writers of the Old Testament were the spokesmen of the community. This is not wholly accurate. Job certainly was not. He rejected the traditional 'hand-out' theology that if a man suffers physically or materially he must have sinned, at least covertly. Jeremiah was not a spokesman of the Jerusalem community. The community did make a contribution, but there was the continual action and inter-action of the individual and his community. Likewise in the New Testament. Paul was not the spokesman of his community. He was the spokesman of the Risen Lord. And it was because the Church in the course of the first centuries saw the books which now make up the New Testament as reflecting genuine apostolic tradition and as an image of what she should be, crystallized under the Spirit, that she received them as sacred and canonical. Before her Israel had done the same. She had seen herself, her experience with God and her traditions reflected in the Pentateuch, in the former prophets, which embraced Joshua to Kings, and in the later prophets. Her Wisdom was found in the Writings.

The Spirit worked in God's community in its formative and preformative stages. The members all in greater or lesser degrees shared in inspiration. Those who wrote in some way for the community, who wrote so as to give some account of God's dealings with man, with his revealing of himself, and whose work was assumed into the text of the Bible as we now have it, shared the charism of scriptural inspiration.

The Canon Settles Itself

At the time when the people of Yahweh became the Church of God the Canon of the Torah and the Prophets was closed. But Israel did not pass on a closed canon of the Writings. This collection of books was somewhat loose. When her canon was finally settled she did not include such books as the Wisdom of Solomon, Ben Sirach (Ecclesiasticus), Tobit, Judith, 1 & 2 Maccabees. But the Spirit of God at work among the Jews of the dispersion and Alexandria gave us the Wisdom of Solomon, the Greek Ben Sirach, Maccabees. The Spirit was even at work in the man who summarized the five books of Jason of Cyrene into what is now the second book of Maccabees, written in that literary form which the French call *histoire pathétique,* not 'pathetic history', but best understood in the sense of the *actio* and *passio* of Aristotle's Poetics or as that *pathetikon* which Cicero describes as *quo perturbantur animi et concitantur* (*Or. ad Brut.* 37). These books, together with Judith, Baruch 1-6, part of Daniel ch. 3, Daniel ch. 13 & 14 (Susanna, Bel and the Dragon), were received into the Christian Church from the earliest times as the reflections of men under the Holy Spirit on God's dealings with his creation and with his chosen people.

The First Vatican Council describes the books of the Bible as being holy and canonical because, written under the inspiring breath of the Holy Spirit, they have God as author and have been handed down to the Church herself as such. Now the Church is not restricted to the pope, bishops, clergy, important and indispensable though their functions are. It comprises all genuinely baptized people of God. In the early centuries of the Church certain books, and these only, had pride of place at the assemblies of the faithful. Though there was a little uncertainty in some places with regard to some of the books, e.g. Hebrews, 1-2 Peter, 2-3 John, Jude, Apocalypse, and some other books as the *Shepherd* of Hermas, 1-2 Clement, the *Didache,* the Letter of Barnabas, were equally venerated in certain churches, the books of the Bible now in use, together with what are known as the deutero-canonical books, were accepted as Scripture by the fourth century. They are listed as such in the Decree of Pope Damasus in 382 A.D. (Dz 179-80). Under the same Spirit that directed their composition, these books imposed themselves upon and were accepted by the Church. Any uncertainty that may have remained for Catholics was dispelled by the Council of Trent with its decree of April 8, 1546 which listed the books of the Bible including the deutero-canonical books (Dz 1502f.).

Inspiration is supernatural and so cannot be diagnosed by historical or literary research. The same Spirit that was at work in the sacred writers of the Old Testament, in the apostles and the apostolic Church is always and is still at work. And we can only repeat the words of Johann von Drey, already cited at the beginning of Chapter Two: 'The faithful preservation of the apostolic writings is the work of the Spirit of God acknowledging his own products.' And these products he has also acknowledged in the pre-Church of the old Testament.

CHAPTER 4

THE TRUTH OF THE BIBLE
PART I

The purpose of inspiration is to record in writing the experience of the believer of God's people with himself, his fellow man, his nation and its history. Because he is a believer he reads out of his experience God's dealings with him. God is giving his revelation, is communicating himself through human means. God is truth communicating truth. The constant conviction of the biblical writers is that God is true to himself and never abandons his creation or his people. His fidelity to himself and his steadfast love move to a climax in the New Testament where the Logos steps into history as Jesus of Nazareth and becomes the glorified Christ. It is in this context that we look for the truth of the Bible.

An expected title of this chapter might have been 'The Inerrancy of the Bible'. But because of its very negative connotations and associations, of its defensive mentality, of the timorous attitude that it displays, I think that it would be better to drop the word 'inerrancy' from the theological vocabulary. The word is not characteristic of ecclesiastical documents.

The Church has always believed that the Bible is true. The Fathers and exegetes have always been aware of the apparent errors and inconsistencies in the Bible. The difficulty which these cause has been well summed up by St Augustine in a letter to St Jerome:

> I acknowledge ...that it is only to those books of Scripture that are now called canonical that I have learned to pay such reverence and respect as to believe most firmly that not one of their authors has made any error. Should I come across anything in these books that seems contrary to truth I

shall have no hesitation in concluding either that the text is faulty or that the translator has not grasped the meaning of the text or that I myself have not understood it (Letter 32; CSEL 34, p. 354).

Augustine saw some of the difficulties that excited the nineteenth-century devotees of strict historicism. He noted that Matthew wrote that the centurion of Capernaum came to Jesus personally (Matt 5.5), while Luke said that the centurion sent 'elders of the Jews' (Lk 7.3). Augustine set out to solve the problem. He was of the opinion that Luke narrated what actually took place, while Matthew used a figure of speech in as much as he asserted that the centurion 'came' to Jesus through others to ask a favour. Augustine also proposed an alternative solution. It was through faith such as is not found in Israel that the centurion came to Jesus. And so Matthew contemplating the depth of the mystery could say that the centurion himself came. Neither Matthew nor Luke is guilty of deception (*De Consensu Evangelistarum,* 2.20, 50; P.L. 34.1100-01).

The Catholic difficulty with inerrancy or, better, with the truth of the Bible is analagous to the difficulty with the Incarnation. God became man like to us in everything except sin. The word incarnate submitted himself to all the limitations of the human condition except that he never for a moment deviated from the path to the Father – such deviation is what sin is. But he suffered, he was disappointed, depressed, misunderstood, rejected; he was angry, he loved, he submitted himself to ignorance, he felt himself abandoned. Otherwise he would not have been man. Catholic tradition has always vigorously maintained the divinity of Jesus. It would be untrue to say that it has even for a moment forgotten the humanity. But much popular devotion and writing and even at times theological writing gives the impression of Docetism, that is that Jesus was either a sort of superman or one who seemed to be subject to human limitations but somehow, because of his divinity, was not. He was a sort of actor. In the face of nineteenth-century rationalism the Church was forced to insist on the divinity of Jesus. The humanity was not forgotten, but it receded into the background. It was similar with the word of God. The Church insisted on the divine origin of Scripture, on the continual divine influence during the process of formation of Scripture. She never forgot the human element, indeed the papal encyclicals point to the characteristic and individuating traits of the human authors which can be detected in the Scriptures. But insistence on the divine origin and action once again tended to obscure the human element, and the starting point of the discussion was the less known divine action rather than the better known human element, namely the books of the Bible themselves and the history of their composition.

The 'inerrancy' problem and the nineteenth century

The problem of the truth of the Bible became critical with the advance of knowledge in the nineteenth century. The sciences of geology, paleontology, archaeology were put on a firm basis, as was scientific history. Each of the specialties checked the Bible against its findings and found 'errors' there. The professional historians like Leopold von Ranke and Theodore Mommsen sought out in the past 'that which actually took place'. Conservative biblicists, Protestant and Catholic alike, accepted the principles of scientific history and applied them to the Bible, as did their secular counterparts. The critical historian found that much information in the Bible, historical, geographical, scientific, was simply 'wrong'. The religious exegete was reduced to defending literally the 'truth' of the Bible, not without some extraordinary gymnastics and, especially in the New Testament, some unrealistic harmonizing. It took quite some time for both parties to realize that the Bible was not 'pure history', that because much of it is a theology of history and because it carries a supernatural message in human language it cannot be measured adequately by the standard of modern historical research.

Church documents and 'error' in the Bible

The Bible was thought to be history as a nineteenth-century historian would have written it. Each of its statements therefore had to be defended as accurate according to these historical criteria. The revelation-theology of the time tended to think that God revealed himself in propositions, and the Bible was too often regarded as a source from which texts were quarried to prove some point of doctrine. Each proposition in the Bible had to be defended. It was in this context that Leo XIII wrote in rather severe terms in *Providentissimus Deus* in 1893:

> For all the books which the Church receives as sacred and canonical are written wholly and entirely with all their parts at the dictation of the Holy Spirit; and so far is it from being possible that any error can co-exist with inspiration, that inspiration not only is essentially incompatible with error, but excludes and rejects it as absolutely and necessarily as it is impossible that God Himself, the supreme Truth, can utter that which is not true (RSS p. 24).

This, says the Pope, is the constant teaching of the Church, and he refers to the Councils of Florence, Trent and the Vatican. God is the author of Scripture. Hence

> it follows that those who maintain that an error is possible in any genuine passage of the sacred writings either pervert the Catholic notion of inspiration or make God the author of such error (*ibid*. p. 25).

The Pope continues that

> ...nothing can be proved either by physical science or archaeology which can really contradict the Scriptures. If, then, apparent contradiction be met with, every effort should be made to remove it (*ibid.* p. 27).

A large part of the exegete's work was to defend. He was engaged in a contest in which he had to show how the truth of the Scriptures prevailed in spite of the advances of modern science and scholarship. Pope Leo writes that '...it must be clearly understood whom we have to oppose and contend against, and what are their tactics and arms.' He names as the chief enemies the Rationalists

> ...true children and inheritors of the older heretics, who, trusting in their own way of thinking, have rejected even the scraps and remnants of Christian belief which have been handed down to them. They deny that there is any such thing as revelation or inspiration or Holy Scriptures at all; they see, instead, only the forgeries and the falsehoods of men; they set down the Scripture narratives as stupid fables and lying stories; the prophecies and the oracles of God are to them either predictions made up after the event or forecasts formed by the light of nature... (*ibid.* p. 10).

There are several paragraphs which aim at equiping defenders of the Scriptures against these enemies. The polemical and defensive tone continues in the encyclical *Spiritus Paraclitus* of Benedict XV, 1920, which followed in the wake of the modernist crisis.

Solutions of the 'inerrancy' problem

a) *The Bible does not teach natural science:*
Leo XIII points out that the writers of Scripture did not

intend to teach the natural sciences, and he quotes Augustine, who wrote that the Holy Spirit 'who spoke by them, did not intend to teach men these things (that is to say, the essential nature of the things of the visible universe), things in no way profitable unto salvation' (*De Genesi ad litt.*, 1,21,41). The cosmology and cosmography of the first creation-account is weird and wonderful. The earth is presumed to be a flat disc resting on the waters, the heavens a solid vault shaped like an up-turned pudding basin and supported by two pillars at the extremities of the earth. There are waters above the vault, whence the rain when God opens the sluice gates as he does to cause the flood (Gen 7.11). There are waters below the earth, whence the springs of water and the rivers. God asked Job on what were the bases of the earth sunk (Job 38.6), and the great prophet of the exile speaks of him 'who sits above the circle of the earth' (Isa 40.22), that is the flat disc floating on the waters. The very first verses of the Bible present God as bringing *kosmos,* order, out of chaos, resuming the theme of primeval darkness and dampness and the violent wind blowing over the deep which was characteristic of the Near Eastern stories of the origins of the world. That was simply the science of the time, and through this medium the theologian of the Priestly tradition made his confession in one God utterly distinct from the so-called deities of the sun, moon and stars of the surrounding cultures. How often had Israel been warned against them, and how often had she succumbed to their allurement (cf. Deut 4.19-20; 2 Kings 18.4; 23.4-7, 10-11).

In the book of Joshua 'the sun stayed in the midst of heaven, and did not hasten to go down for about a whole day' (10.13). In this and the preceding verses we have a poetic and a poetic-prose account of the same event. And if that is the way the men of the time thought the universe revolved or did not revolve, then be it so! They obviously believed it. In the encyclical Leo XIII says that the writers did not seek to penetrate nature, 'but rather described and dealt with things in more or less figurative language, or in terms which were commonly used at the time...' They 'went by what sensibly appeared.' Now this is true. And it is equally true that they were not teaching astronomy or cosmology. Yet their framework was what we would call factually and scientifically wrong. But through it, now in epic style, now in a rhythmic *credo,* they confessed God as faithful to his people and to his creation. It worries us little these days that the natural science of the Bible was wrong. We know that its message is religious and that the authors spoke as men of their times.

b) *The Bible and history*

Leo XIII wrote that the principles he had enunciated regarding 'what sensibly appeared' and popular speech will apply especially to history. Some exegetes spoke of 'history according to appearances' or popular history. There were some gauche applications of this analogy and they drew some rather negative remarks from Benedict XV:

> And if Leo XIII does say that we can apply to history and cognate subjects the same principles which hold good for science, he yet does not lay this down as a universal law, but simply says that we can apply a like line of argument when refuting the fallacies of adversaries and defending the historical truth of Scripture from their assaults (RSS p. 53).

Statements in Scripture had to be defended at all cost.

Rather than decide what sort of history should be in the Bible, let us go to the books themselves and try to discover what is actually there. The first eleven chapters of Genesis cannot be classed as history in any modern sense of the word. But they are not meaningless fable. They are 'The Book of the Origins', the origin of evil, of

God's people, the initiative of God's steadfast love. As we saw in Chapter Three, they repeat four times the terrible fact of man's helplessness when left to himself. Man, that is the meaning of the Hebrew word 'adam, and woman decide to be a law unto themselves, to be independent of God; disaster follows, and God is presented as moving in to save and protect man from his own foolishness. Cain usurps the law to himself; he is punished, but God sets a protecting mark on him. Mankind in general abandons God, as we read in the prelude to the Flood narrative. Punishment follows, but God's saving arm is there. The builders of the Tower of Babel will be independent of God and confusion follows, but God saves through one who comes from the very land of Babel itself, Abraham. All these stories are saturated with the mythology, folklore, traditions, general cultural heritage of the ancient Near East and are narrated through this medium. We should not be surprised at this. Rather we should expect it. The patriarchal stories, legends and sagas, and there are not many of them, are gathered around three names, Abraham, Isaac and Jacob. Their historical background is clearly the first half of the second millenium B.C. Though the stories are rooted in history, like any good historical novel, one does not defend their historicity. They are religious stories which have their origins in the dim past but which have been developed and reflected upon to show God's fidelity to the people he has chosen. They were given their present form probably when the monarchy was at its height and the religious writers would appreciate from the viewpoint of the vast extent of the Davidic kingdom the hand of God which had formed a nation from a few scattered tribes and a few nondescript free-booters. At times the writers are not quite sure to which patriarch some of the traditions are to be attached and what are the circumstances surrounding the tradition. In Gen 12.10-20 we read that Abram and his wife Sarai went down to Egypt during a famine. The Patriarch had told Sarai to say that she was his sister, otherwise the Egyptians, seeing that she was very beautiful, would do away with him and keep her for themselves. The Egyptians took her to Pharoah's house and a plague came upon it because of Sarai. She then announced that she was Abram's wife. Pharoah gave her back and ordered Abram to leave with her. In Gen 20.1-20 the story is told of Abraham and Sarah; their names had now been changed (cf. Gen 17.5,15). On this occasion they go down to the Negeb. Abraham had used the same ploy, 'She is my sister.' The villain of the piece is Abimelech king of Gerar. He took Sarah. During the night he was visited by God who revealed to him that the woman was Abraham's wife. Next morning Abimelech was quick to summon Abraham and ask what he meant by this deception and restore his wife. In Gen. 26.6-11 the story is told of Isaac and Rebekah. They went down to Gerar and again the patriarch presented his wife as his sister to the annoyance of Abimelech. What is the historical truth? What actually happened? Are the three stories true or only one or two of them? That is not the way the writers of the ancient Near East thought. There were several traditions in circulation of God's providential care in preserving the ancestors of the race. Probably too the stories, especially the first one, celebrate the astuteness of the patriarch and the beauty of his wife, the ancestress of the Israelites. The final redactor-author of Genesis simply set these traditions down more or less side by side. These are the traditions of God's loving care for our people at its origins, he says. And we could proceed likewise through the Joseph narrative and unravel the two strands of narrative preserving two different traditions of his being sold into Egypt.

We have already mentioned the historical chronicle of Samuel and Kings in Chapter Three. There accurate state archives are used as reference points and they are combined with conflicting traditions regarding the monarchy (1 Sam 8-12), varying accounts of the death of Saul (1 Sam 31 & 2 Sam 1), cycles of stories, legends and anecdotes, the Elijah Cycle (1 Kings 17-2 Kings 1), the Elisha Cycle (2 Kings 2-13). All is interpreted and presented within a definite pattern of religious history, fidelity or infidelity to the Deuternomic law. The history we read in the Old Testament is not just popular history. It is religious history understood within a definite framework which incorporates popular stories and legends together with much that is fairly accurate reporting of history, e.g. the Court History of David (2 Sam 9-20; 1 Kings 1-2).

c) *Literary Forms:*

If we were to read an anthology of English literature from Chaucer to the present day comprising poetry, drama, prose, oratory, historical and philosophical writing as if all were history of some sort, we would scarcely do justice to literature and would misunderstand most of it. Now the Bible contains many different literary types covering about one thousand years. We must be sure that we understand what type of literature we are dealing with in each book and what diverse forms are used within the compass of one book. The study of the literary types of the Bible owes much to the great German scholars Hermann Gunkel and Hugo Gressmann whose first uses of the method were published in the period 1890-1910. Not only did they make use of the results of Near Eastern archaeology and general studies related to the Near East, but they also applied the methods of comparative literature to the Old Testament. They viewed Old Testament literature within the framework of ancient Near Eastern literature as a whole. Gunkel based his study of literary types on the assumption that the rhetorical forms and literary types were more fixed than they are today and, as it were, imposed themselves on the writer. If a poet or writer wished to speak or write on a certain theme then he did it in a certain fixed way. Individual forms and formulas became highly stylized. Now this is all true and was a major contribution to the study of the Bible. But one must remember that literary forms and form-criticism are tools for the understanding of the Bible and not tyrannical masters. There were naturally enough exaggerations in the use of this new-found tool. Form and the content of a literary unit do not always agree, and to apply form criticism beyond the original literary or rhetorical unit to phrases or to whole books can often lead to distortion. It was into this context of literary types, still in its infancy and not well understood by so many, that Benedict XV wrote of those who

> ...take too ready a refuge in such notions as 'implicit quotations' or 'pseudo-historical narratives', or in 'kinds of literature' *(genera quaedam litterarum)* in the Bible such as cannot be reconciled with the entire and perfect truth of God's word... (RSS p. 54).

But one does not take refuge in a literary form. One just does not communicate without a 'form' or 'type', literary or oral. It was in 1943 in his encyclical *Divino Afflante Spiritu* that Pius XII officially recognized how indispensable was this approach to the Bible. Not only must the exegete know and make use of the history, archaeology, ethnology, languages of the ancient Near East; he must by these means 'discover what literary forms the writers of that early age intended to use, and did in fact employ... and what these were the exegete cannot determine *a priori,* but only from a careful study of ancient oriental literature.' These literary forms were used '...in poetical descriptions, or in the formulation of rules and laws of conduct, or in the narration of historical facts and events.' Above all the exegete should bear in mind '...the special purpose, the religious purpose, of biblical history.' No literary forms are excluded 'so long as they are in no way incompatible with God's sanctity and truth.' Yet in the midst of this very positive approach we have echoes of the defensive mentality which characterized previous ecclesiastical documents when we read that '...a knowledge and careful appreciation of ancient modes of expression and literary forms and styles will provide a solution to many of the objections made against the truth and historical accuracy of Holy Writ...' (cf. Pius XII, *Biblical Studies,* C.T.S. nos. 38-42).

While we must remember that the encyclical is not an essay in literary criticism, nevertheless a few remarks on literature and literary types are in order. A literary form is not, I think, something that one can choose or not choose to adopt. One writes in some form and there is no form which is not a stylization. The whole man expresses himself through the form. It is not partly man, partly form. The style is the man. We must not equate the style merely with kinds of embellishments, with terseness, prolixity, continued metaphor, insistent parallelism.

These features are indices of something deeper and more pervasive. The literary form may well be thought of a something analagous to the substantial form in scholastic philosophy. It has no reality except when informing, and is all-determining when doing so.

Our customary discourse is prosaic and we are inclined to forget how very much prose, particularly when written, differs from ordinary speech when we exclaim, utter disconnected sentences or half sentences and assorted noises, all accompanied by gesture, intonation and facial expression. But when we listen to a skilled and serious speaker dealing with a topic that engages him, we become aware how his own personality takes possession of the language. When we have an outstanding piece of writing like *The Canterbury Tales* or *Hamlet,* we might at first be tempted to separate out the element into message, import, travel-cycle, revenge-tragedy, styl-izations, decorations, the writer's distinctive intonations. But it is not possible to distinguish these adequately from one another. And the attempt to give precedence to the message, for example, over the others, must be very delicate when the work is of any degree of sophistica-tion. A literary form is not like the skin of an orange which one peels off to get at what really matters. It is not like a shirt which, dexterously removed, leaves the truth exposed to our gaze in all its nakedness.

When *Divino Afflante Spiritu* says that the ancients used the forms and expressions current among the peo-ple of their own time and place, this is true and impor-tant. But the reader must go further. He must see how the writer takes possession of these forms, how he makes them his own and adapts them to his purpose and needs. By way of antithesis we can also speak of the writer *being used* by the forms. They are traditional, and he will naturally fall into them as he writes. And so we have action and interaction. Writing too is a process of discovery, of 'seeing what the world has to say about what you have to say about it.' And the dominant form will be the overall form of attention. It is useful for the reader to know these different forms. He will be able to say that it is this or that, not that other one. But then he must proceed further and find out what the work as a whole is.

The broad lines of the story of Job were traditional. A wealthy and prosperous man had lost all his material possessions and had suffered injury to his person. He endured this with patience and without any sinful utter-ance against God. His patience was rewarded with resto-ration of property and health. Into this framework is in-serted the classic which we read as the book of Job. One from the group that takes the view that scientific or phi-losophical or 'obvious' truth is primary may well have summed up the message: God is unteachable and incomprehensible; man must simply accept this and bow before his maker. But in that case we would not have the book of Job. The author of Job struggles to this truth through searing dialogue and monologue in which he rejects the traditional 'hand-out' theology and its answers and makes a personal effort to penetrate a problem ever ancient and ever new. And he draws his reader through this same experience. Imaginative writing is as apt to express the unteachableness and incomprehensibility of God as is the cold philosophical statement. One cannot treat Job either as theology or as literature. It is both. It is a masterpiece of theological or religious literature and the theology is presented and experienced as literature.

The theologians' approach to truth in the Bible has been far too scientific-philosophical. It is useful to sum up the 'message' of a work of literature in a brief sentence, but the truth of the work is not limited to this summary. One takes whatever truth one can get in whatever way one can get it. And one final remark. The encyclical says that no literary forms are excluded from the Bible so long as they are not incompatible with God's sanctity and truth. It is not easy to grasp what is meant here. A literary form or type is a poetic or prose way of expressing something either in writing or in speech. It is difficult to see how a way of communicating could ever be incompatible with divine truth. Behind the statement there seems to be the notion that one can separate the form from the content in literature.

d) *Myths:*

The *Oxford English Dictionary* describes myth as 'a purely fictitious narrative usually involving supernatural persons, actions or event, and embodying some popular idea concerning natural or historical phenomena.' This is a rather academic description, however much truth it may contain. For Old Testament study it is better not to build our description of myth on theoretical considerations or even on the universal phenomenology of religions. We mean by myth something such as is found in the Gilgamesh epic or in the mythological texts of Ras Shamra. And Pritchard's *Ancient Near Eastern Texts* give us an idea of the tremendous amount of mythological material from the ancient Near East. Much of this was part of Israel's cultural heritage and was at hand to prophets and poets to illustrate or enliven their narratives, e.g. Amos 9.3; Isaiah 14.12ff. The Israelites appropriated many Canaanite and Mesopotamian myths, one of the most prominent being that of the powers of the primeval chaos. These powers, forces, dragons, personified monsters were in Israel always subordinated to Yahweh as we read in Isaiah 51.9-10 and Ps 74.13; it is the Lord who splits Rahab in two and crushes the head of Leviathan. Again in the myth of the 'sons of god' in Gen 6.1-4 we see their activities subordinated to the judgment of Yahweh. Mythological allusions and mythological motifs are legion in the Old Testament; but Israel did not borrow myth unchanged; she subsumed it under the transcendence of Yahweh. It is not so much 'Whatever they can do, Yahweh can do better,' but rather 'Say what you will, Yahweh is supreme'. Israel did not create her own myths simply because she was monotheistic. Her use of mythological motifs is subordinate and illustrative: subordinate – that is, the themes are always dominated by her steadfast faith in one God; illustrative – the themes are, as it were, so many dramatic canvases on which to picture the universal supremacy of Yahweh.

Myth is above all a way of thinking, it is an attempt in some way to grasp the truth. This is well expressed by Fr Roderick MacKenzie:

Myth is always an attempt to express, and thereby to make comprehensible, some truth about the world and man's existence in it, a truth inaccessible and unknown in itself, but capable of being ex-

pressed in and by symbols. It is not of the essence
of myth that it be polytheistic, telling stories about
gods and goddesses. What is essential is that it
should attempt to formulate transcendental reality,
to reach something behind the flux of phenomena
that envelops human existence, to pin down an absolute in which the human mind can rest with
some feeling of security (*Faith and History in the
Old Testament,* Univ. of Minnesota Press, 1963,
pp. 63-4).

The encyclical *Humani Generis,* 1950, of Pius XII refers back to the letter of the Biblical Commission to Cardinal Suhard, 16 January 1948, dealing with the Pentateuch and especially with the early chapters of Genesis.
These chapters

have a simple, symbolical way of speaking suited
to the understanding of a not very sophisticated
people... It may be granted that the ancient writers
of history may have drawn on popular stories; but
it must be remembered that they did so with the
helping breath of divine inspiration which shielded
them from all error in selecting from and assessing
those documents.

The exerpts from popular stories which are found
in the sacred books must not be equated with my-
thologies and the like. These myths flow from the
outpouring of the imagination rather than from
that love of truth and simplicity which so shines
out even in the sacred books of the Old Testament
as to put their authors on a clearly different level
from their profane contemporaries. (Dz 3898-9:
the translation has made use of that made for the
Tablet by the late Ronald A. Knox).

When the encyclical speaks of 'a simple, symbolical way
of speaking' what is said is quite true, but can be misleading. No contemporary student of the nature of
myth and of the mythopoeic imagination would think

myth a cruder form of attention to, or formulation of, reality than, say, philosophical or scientific thinking. Certain things told about the origins of the world can't be told in any other way than that of Genesis. And we must put up with it. And one must insist too that when one says that something is symbolic, one ought not say that it is only a symbol. Symbols which are only symbols are not symbols.

Some years ago I read the statement on myth from *Humani Generis,* without giving any indication of its source, to a group of academics to whom I was giving a series of seminars on the book of Genesis. The group comprised people of different faiths, of no faith and agnostics. They were graduates and specialists in literature, history, psychology, sociology and science. None would accept this description of myth. And rightly so. The background of the description is that of the *a priori* scholastic philosopher and not of the historian of religion where myth is found. One can affirm through scientific history. One can affirm no less and in no less godly wise by blending conjecture, mythopoeic imagination, dream, as is done in much of the Bible. And it is difficult to establish that the authors of *Enuma Elish,* for example, have less love of truth and any less cult of simplicity than those of Genesis. A love of truth is not bound up with a cult of simplicity and what is one man's simplicity may be another's dexterity.

The encyclical concedes, not very readily, that the biblical writers may have used stories current in their day. But this, it continues, they did under divine inspiration. This could be misleading. It is not as though the writer were dictating his book and then suddenly, under impulse from above, he seized on a current story to illustrate his point. All men of the ancient Near East of any education were familiar with the traditional myths and legends. They would refer to them quite naturally. The Holy Spirit takes men *completely* as they are and works in them as in faith they subordinate all to the providence of a one true God.

e) *The New Testament and 'error'*
The New Testament has caused real difficulties in the matter of 'error'. It is notoriously impossible to harmonize the Passion and Resurrection narratives. The impression is given by Luke that all the events of Ch. 24 including the Ascension took place on the day of the Resurrection. Acts mentions the forty days between the Resurrection and Ascension. It is just as impossible to reconcile such comparatively simple and straightforward narratives as the accounts of the death of Judas in Matthew 27.1-10 and Acts 1.16-20. In Matthew Judas hanged himself, in Acts 'becoming prone [falling headlong? did he throw himself over a cliff?] he burst asunder.' In Matthew the priests bought the field, in Acts Judas 'gained possession of a field with the proceeds of his crime.' In Matthew the field is called the field of blood because it was the burial place for strangers, in Acts it takes its name from Judas' suicide in it. Do we force these accounts into a unity to avoid attributing inaccuracy to the Holy Spirit? The Second Vatican Council, following previous ecclesiastical statements, writes that '...everything asserted by the inspired authors or sacred writers must be held to be asserted by the Holy Spirit...' May we ask then what the authors of Matthew and Acts are asserting? Presumably that this is the tradition about the death of Judas that each has received and that each is recording his tradition accurately. Examples could be multiplied indefinitely, e.g., the blind man at Jericho in Luke 18.35-43; Matt 20.29-34; Mark 10.46-52. Were there two blind men or only one? Did Jesus perform the miracle when entering or when leaving Jericho? A large part of the great discourse of Mark 13, given a few days before the Passion, is found in Matthew 10, in a missionary address to the disciples. The gospels are primari-

ly religious or theological documents which are rooted in history. The *Constitution on Revelation* of the Second Vatican Council says that the Church has always unhesitatingly asserted their 'historical character' *(historicitas),* and that they 'faithfully hand on what Jesus Christ, while living among men, really did and taught for their eternal salvation.' 'Historical character' or *historicitas* means relating to history; the words and events recorded have a real connection with the historical Jesus. After the events the Resurrection-Ascension, a period which Jesus spent 'speaking of the kingdom of God' (Acts 1.3), the Holy Spirit came on the first Christian Pentecost. It was with that clearer understanding which was the result of these events that the sacred authors wrote the four gospels,

> selecting some things from the many which had been handed on by word of mouth or in writing, reducing some of them to a synthesis, explicating *(explanantes)* some things in view of the situation of their churches, and preserving the form of proclamation but always in such fashion that they told the honest truth about Jesus (*Dogmatic Constitution on Divine Revelation,* n. 19).

And the purpose was that 'we might know "the truth" concerning those matters about which we have been instructed.' What this truth is we shall now discuss.

CHAPTER 5

THE TRUTH OF THE BIBLE
PART II

Theologians and Church documents have defended the
'inerrancy' of the Bible on three fronts. Firstly, it was
pointed out that the Bible does not teach natural science
and so it is not in conflict with the discoveries of modern
science. Secondly, biblical history is popular history and
is not written according to the scholarly canons of the
modern western world. Thirdly, one must understand
the literary forms of the Bible. Now all this is perfectly
true and a proper appreciation of it all is quite indispensable for a correct understanding of the Bible. But neither individually nor taken together do these defences
give us a panacea for the inerrancy problem. They take
us a certain necessary distance and no more. And they
should be borne in mind when reading any ancient literature, and modern literature for that matter; they are not
peculiar to the Bible.

The consequence of inspiration is not inerrancy but
truth. The truth we look for in the Bible is not the *adae-
quatio rei et intellectus* (correspondence of intellect and
reality) of scholastic philosophy nor Descartes' 'that
which is clearly and distinctly perceived'. The truth of
the Bible is not philosophical truth, nor is it found in a
series of propositions. For the Semite in general and the
Israelite in particular truth, *'emet,* has many nuances:
firmness, faithfulness, stability, continuance, reliability,
etc. (cf. Brown-Driver-Briggs, *A Hebrew and English
Lexicon of the Old Testament,* O.U.P.). Truth, *'emet,* is
often linked with or parallel with *hesed,* which described
Yahweh's steadfast love. And the truth and steadfast
love of Yahweh remain for ever (Pss 117.2; 146.2; cf.
Ex 34.6). As Walther Zimmerli has very well written:

> The history of the Old Testament derives its form
> from a single fundamental fact, namely that in
> the course of the unique and astonishing historical
> event of being liberated under Moses' leadership
> Israel experienced the summons of Yahweh, and
> this summons was proclaimed to her in that histor-
> ical event (O. Loretz, *The Truth of Bible,* Burns &
> Oates 1968, pp. 46-7).

This saving act is understood in the Scriptures in the
context of God's covenant with his people. God will always be faithful to his covenant and he demands like fidelity from his people. And prophets continually rise up
in Israel to remind the people of this. The Old Testament is a constant presentation of God as true to his
promise and his word. 'The grass withers, the flower
fades; but the word of our God will stand for ever' (Is
40.8). And the New Testament witnesses to the consummation of this fidelity. The truth of the Bible is the truth,
steadfastness, constancy of God to himself, to his people
and to his creation.

The Constitution of Vatican II on Revelation, and truth

'Truth' and 'the true' are a *leitmotif* of the Second Vatican Council's *Constitution on Revelation.* The theme occurs some nineteen times. The purpose of the document
is 'to set forth authentic teaching about divine revelation
and about how it is handed on' (Preface). God has revealed himself through deeds and words in the history of
salvation and by this revelation 'the deepest truth about
God and the salvation of man is made clear to us in
Christ' (ch. 1, n. 2). During the period of preparation in
the Old Testament God, through the patriarchs, Moses
and the prophets, taught his people 'to acknowledge
Himself as the one living and true God...' (ch. 1, n.3).
And Jesus perfected this revelation by his life and teach-

ing and above all through his death and resurrection 'and final sending of the Spirit of truth' (ch. 1, n. 4). Man commits himself freely to God in an obedience of faith, 'freely assenting to the truth revealed by him' (ch. 1, n. 5). The Holy Spirit precedes and operates in this whole process of faith.

God willed that this revelation be handed on to all mankind in its integrity. And so Christ in whom the revelation reaches its consummation commissioned the apostles to preach 'that gospel which is the source of all saving truth and moral teaching' (ch. 2, n. 7). The phrase 'saving truth' is taken from the Council of Trent which uses it in a similar context. The commission was fulfilled by the apostles in their oral teaching and by both the apostles and others under their aegis who under the breath of the Spirit committed the message of salvation to writing.

The Scriptures are apostolic tradition committed to writing; they refer to what has been handed down and to what those who receive the traditions must in their turn pass on. Under the Spirit there will be a constant, gradual and more intimate understanding of the revelation to which 'those who have received through episcopal succession the sure gift of truth' (ch. 2, n. 8) will make a contribution. The Church thus 'moves forward towards the fullness of divine truth until the words of God reach their complete fulfilment in her' *(ibid.)* There is continual dialogue between the Son and the Church he founded. The Holy Spirit who guides this dialogue 'leads unto all truth those who believe and makes the word of Christ dwell abundantly in them' *(ibid.).*

Scripture and tradition are intimately linked as they flow from the same wellspring. Scripture is the word of God in as much as it is consigned to writing under the Spirit. Tradition hands on to the successors of the apostles the word of God and they 'led by the light of the Spirit of truth..., can in their preaching preserve this word of God faithfully, explain it, and make it more widely known' (ch. 2, n. 9).

The document continues that there are 'divinely revealed realities which are contained and presented in sacred Scripture.' Because this took place under the inspiration of the Holy Spirit, the Scriptures have God as their author.

> Therefore, since everything asserted by the inspired authors or sacred writers must be held to be asserted by the Holy Spirit, it follows that the books of Scripture must be acknowledged as teaching firmly, faithfully, and without error that truth which God wanted put into the sacred writings for the sake of our salvation (ch. 3, n. 11).

God has used weak humanity to convey his message, yet 'the truth and holiness of God always remains intact' (ch. 3, n. 13).

In treating of the Old Testament in detail the council repeats that God 'manifested Himself through words and deeds as the one true and living God...', and that the plan of salvation foretold, recounted and explained by the sacred authors 'is found as the true word of God in the books of the Old Testament' (ch. 4, n. 14).

The Word Incarnate of the New Testament 'dwelt among us in the fullness of grace and truth' (ch. 5, n. 17). The gospels which witness to him were written 'by the light of the Spirit of truth' who enabled the apostolic writers, in the light of the Easter and Pentecost experience, to penetrate more deeply what Christ is, said, and did. They tell us 'the honest truth about Jesus.' They were written, as Luke tells us in his preface, that 'we might know "the truth" concerning those matters about which we have been instructed' (ch. 5, n. 19).

The final reference in the document to truth is in the context of theology. The basis of theology is the written word of God and tradition. 'By scrutinizing in the light of faith all truth stored up in the mystery of Christ, theology is most powerfully strengthened and constantly rejuvenated by that word' (ch. 6, n. 24).

The whole thrust of the constitution is towards explaining that the truth of revelation has been preserved. It did not easily find this direction, as we shall see. The council did not attempt to define precisely the historical truth of the Old Testament. With regard to the New Testament, it insists that it has a real connection with the historical Jesus and presents the honest truth about him. It does not define this truth further.

The Constitution on Revelation and the truth of Scripture

The Second Vatican Council moved slowly and painfully to its final and penetrating description of the truth of the Bible. The draft schema which was circulated among the bishops before the first session in 1962 had been already revised twice. This third edition spoke of the 'absolute inerrancy' of Scripture in very strong terms:

> Because divine inspiration extends to everything, it is a direct and necessary consequence that the whole of Sacred Scripture is absolutely free from error. The ancient and constant faith of the Church teaches us that it is utterly unlawful to admit that the sacred writer has erred, since divine inspiration of its nature excludes and rejects all error in any matter, religious or profane, with that same necessity that God, the Supreme Truth, can be the source of no error whatsoever.

The document continued that it was the constant conviction of the Church that the Bible excluded error in the whole ambit of religious and profane statements. The word 'inerrancy' occured in the title of the chapter. The document was severely criticized by many of the bishops, and Pope John finally withdrew it and appointed a new and more representative commission to prepare an entirely new schema in the light of the criticisms made. The new draft did not have the word 'inerrancy' in the chapter-heading. The purpose of the chapter was that we should 'see clearly what truth God wanted to communicate to us.' The pertinent sentence read: 'Since, therefore, God is affirmed to be and is the principal author of the whole of Scripture, it follows that the whole of divinely inspired Scripture is utterly free from any error.' This draft was not discussed at the second session in 1963, but the bishops were able to submit their written observations on it to the competent commission. As a result a further draft, the fifth, was presented to the third session in 1964. The formulation was more positive: '...the books of Scripture as a whole and with all their parts must be acknowledged as teaching truth without error.' The emphasis on truth was a distinct gain, though the formula was something of a tautology. Truth is necessarily free from error, and if a teaching is free from error it is true. Several bishops, notably Cardinals König and Meyer, pointed to a number of factual errors in the Scriptures, that is to errors in matters 'profane'. Consequently the following formula was worked out:

Therefore, since everything asserted by the inspired authors or sacred writers must be held to be asserted by the Holy Spirit, it follows that the books of Scripture must be acknowledged as teaching firmly, faithfully and without error the truth of salvation.

Scripture is aimed at truth, the truth of salvation *(veritas salutaris)*. This formula was passed in the general vote in the fourth session in 1965. However, a number of bishops feared that the document by stating that the Scriptures taught 'salutary truth' without error was placing secular truth, historical truth, outside saving truth or was even denying it to the Bible. The commission replied that by using the expression, which is found in

Trent, it was speaking positively. The religious teaching that concerned our salvation was necessarily free from error. It was not speaking exclusively and had no intention of excluding secular or historical truth from the Bible. There was further discussion, and even a suggestion from Pope Paul himself that the phrase 'saving truth' be omitted not because it was wrong, but because it could well lead to misunderstanding. It might give a lever to some to separate saving truth from history. But the commission did not wish to go back on its insistence on saving truth. Finally there emerged from this prolonged struggle a statement that was at the same time more profound and more satisfying theologically:

> ...the books of Scripture must be acknowledged as teaching firmly, faithfully and without error that truth which God wanted put into the sacred writings for the sake of our salvation.

And this is the Council's final statement on the truth of Scripture. God will communicate to us the truth which is necessary for our salvation. Part of this truth is, for example, the 'profane' fact that Jesus of Nazareth died by crucifixion in Jerusalem under the Roman governor, Pontius Pilate. This is at the same time saving truth, as this Jesus was known by faith to be God made man who, following the will of the Father, offered himself for all men for the forgiveness of sins and the reconciliation of mankind.

The Bible, a witness to God's fidelity

The Bible, then, is a witness to and a true record of God's fidelity to what he is and to the conviction of his people that he will never abandon them. This fidelity is shown through the long centuries during which the books of the Old Testament were formed, each book correcting, modifying other books and redirecting its readers towards God's final manifestation of his fidelity. This fidelity, truth, *'emet,* is revealed in God becoming one of us. He is a God who cares, who has come to us as man to lead us to our final destiny which is God in Christ (Eph 1.3-14). For man to reach God, God has come to man. Human problems, the problem of suffering, are not solved by the Incarnation, but the Incarnation is the guarantee in history and in faith that God cares. He cares so much for men that he has become man with all man's limitations except sin; that does not mean except trial, temptation, anxiety, depression, ignorance and the like. It means what it says, like to us in everything except deviation in any way from the path to God. The New Testament is witness to this. The Spirit who attested Christ (1 Tim 3.16), who communicates the life of Christ (cf. 2 Cor 3.17; Rom 8), moved men to proclaim this event, to live it, to record it. In the Spirit which was given to the Church the first generation of Christians under the apostles and eye-witnesses of the great happening recalled, reflected on, interpreted, adapted and applied to their needs the words and miracles of Jesus. Paul reflected on the great redemptive event, expounded it, drew consequences from it in his letters. It is in this context that we look for the inspiration of the books of the Bible, and it is this great truth of God's fidelity to his covenant in Christ that is taught for the sake of our salvation.

A further contribution

One of the most constructive contributions to the study of the truth of Scripture has been made by my contemporary and friend Fr Norbert Lohfink of the Pontifical Biblical Institute, Rome. He has set out his idea in three articles in German. His proposals are in many ways similar to what has been said in parts of these pages, though

I do not wish to burden him with my own effusions.

Lohfink insists that there can never be a completely abstract and timeless formulation of the teaching on inspiration. When we speak of inerrancy we can speak of (i) the inerrancy of the hagiographer, (ii) the inerrancy of the biblical books, (iii) the inerrancy of the Bible. It is to the last of these three that we should apply inerrancy, to the Bible as a whole. And it is only when the Bible is complete and unified that it is inerrant. Individual books and passages correct and modify other books and passages. There has been a continual attempt to unify the Bible, e.g. the latest additions to Deuteronomy, 4.25-31; 30.1-10. The meaning of the Bible changes with the addition of each book and as long as the canon of the Old Testament can change, no single book can be said to have had its final hagiographer and to have achieved its inerrant meaning and expression. It is the New Testament that gives the Old Testament its final form. Lohfink concludes by quoting Hugh of St Victor: *'Omnis Scriptura unus liber est, et ille unus liber Christus est* (the whole of Scripture is one book, and that one book is Christ).'

A Christological interpretation of the Bible is essential. The Old Testament must be interpreted both historically and Christologically, and if each interpretation is followed to its end, they will meet. The literal sense of any passage is of course what the author intended. But that is not necessarily the inerrant sense. The inerrant sense is to be found only in the context of the complete unity of the Bible.

The emphasis on the truth and unity of the Bible is a distinct gain, and insistence on its whole Christological drive is a debt that we owe to what is best in patristic and medieval exegesis.

It should be clear that the discussion of the inspiration of the Bible moves between two poles: 1) the conviction in faith that the Holy Spirit acts in the many writers who have contributed to the Bible, 2) that the books of the Bible have had a long history of formation. The writer(s) of a biblical book is not like the Egyptian scribe Ra-messe-naki of the nineteenth Dynasty (1320-1200 B.C.) whose statue we see in the Cairo museum. He is seated cross-legged with the papyrus on his knee and a baboon, the emblem of Thoth, the god of learning, on his head. The god whispers wisdom into the scribe's ear. The biblical writer receives no dictation. He uses every faculty that a man normally uses in writing and the Spirit respects his person entirely.

Scriptural inspiration ceases with the writing of the last book of the New Testament canon. But the inspiring breath of the Spirit continues in the Church. It is through the Spirit that she recognized the books of the canon and that she continues and will always continue to see yet other facets of God reveaing himself as true to himself and have fresh insights into the depths of the mystery that he is.

Alonso-Schökel, Luis: *The Inspired Word,* New York: Herder & Herder, 1965. Discusses inspiration from the standpoint of literature and modern hermeneutics.

Bea, Augustin: *The Word of God and Mankind,* London: Geoffrey Chapman, 1967. ch. 7 & 8 discuss Scripture as an inspired and infallible guide and its interpretation.

Benoit, Pierre: *Prophecy and Inspiration,* New York: Desclée, 1961. A commentary on St Thomas on 'Prophecy' with further developments in the light of modern study.

Inspiration and the Bible, London: Sheed & Ward, (paperback) 1965. Developments of the theses in the former title in the light of criticism and discussion.

Burthchaell, J.T.: *Catholic Theories of Biblical Inspiration since 1810,* C.U.P., 1969. A comprehensive study of the history of the problem.

Butler, B.C.: 'Revelation and Inspiration' in *The Theology of Vatican II,* London: Darton, Longman & Todd, 1967.

Lagrange, M.-J.: *Historical Criticism and the Old Testament,* London: C.T.S., 1906. A remarkable work for the period with much that the modern can learn.

Loretz, O.: *The Truth of the Bible,* London/New York: Burns Oates/Herder & Herder, 1968. A positive approach to the problem of 'inerrancy' making much use of Pannenberg's contribution on revelation.

McCarthy, Dennis (edd.) & Callen, William: *Modern Biblical Studies,* Milwaukee: Bruce, 1967. Contains the contributions of McCarthy on 'social inspiration' and of Lohfink on 'inerrancy.'

McKenzie, J.L.: *Myths and Realities,* Milwaukee: Bruce, 1963. A discussion of 'social inspiration.'

Newman. J.H.: *On the Inspiration of Scripture,* (edd. J. Derek Holmes and Robert Murray), London: Geoffrey Chapman, 1967. Newman's two essays on inspiration with a very good introduction.

Rahner, Karl: 'Inspiration in the Bible' in (K. Rahner) *Studies in Modern Theology,* London: Burns Oates, 1965. This is a better translation than that in the series *Quaestiones Disputatae.*

Vorgrimler, H. (ed.): *Commentary on the Documents of Vatican II,* Vol. 3, London/New York: Burns & Oates/Herder & Herder, 1969.

INDEX

95